REAL ESTATE INVESTING WITH LEASE OPTIONS

HOW TO INVEST IN REAL ESTATE WITH NO MONEY DOWN

JIM PELLERIN

Updated for 2023.

Copyright © 2019 by **Realty Investment Seminars & Education**. All Rights Reserved.

No part of this publication may be reproduced, distributed, or transmitted in any form or by any means, including photocopying, recording, or other electronic or mechanical methods, or by any information storage and retrieval system without the prior written permission of the publisher, except in the case of very brief quotations embodied in critical reviews and certain other noncommercial uses permitted by copyright law.

TABLE OF CONTENTS

WHY YOU SHOULD READ THIS BOOK 4

WHY I WROTE THIS BOOK 7

WHAT IS A LEASE OPTION INVESTMENT 9

CHAPTER 1. THE REAL NOTHING DOWN DEAL 13

CHAPTER 2. THE DIFFERENT TYPES OF LEASE OPTIONS 29

CHAPTER 3. ACQUIRING A PROPERTY 41

CHAPTER 4. MAKING MONEY WITH LEASE OPTIONS 57

CHAPTER 5. FINDING TENANT BUYERS 69

CHAPTER 6. FINDING MOTIVATED SELLERS 85

CHAPTER 7. TENANT FINANCING 101

CHAPTER 8. WHAT TYPES OF CONTRACTS DO YOU USE? 115

CHAPTER 9. MANAGING A LEASE OPTION 133

CHAPTER 10. GETTING THE TENANT APPROVED 147

CHAPTER 11. EXIT STRATEGIES 161

CHAPTER 12. CONCLUSION 177

ABOUT THE AUTHOR 181

OTHER BOOKS BY JIM PELLERIN 183

Why You Should Read This Book

Most people get into Real Estate Investing, not because they want to be a Real Estate Investor, but because they want to make money. But most people don't know where to start or don't have the cash to get started in Real Estate Investing.

This book provides you will all the strategies you would need to get started in Real Estate Investing <u>without using any of your own money</u>. There are a lot of books out there that claim to show you how to get started in Real Estate Investing with no money down. But none of them, that I have found, focuses specifically on Lease Options as a strategy to do that.

In this book, you will learn the various ways you can acquire properties using none of your own money. You will learn the different types of Lease Option strategies and when to use each one. You will learn the different ways to make money in each Lease Option transaction. You will also learn the different types of exit strategies and how to protect yourself from losing money when you sell.

I will describe the different contracts that you can use when setting up a Lease Option transaction.

You will also learn that the most significant factor in successful Lease Option Investing is motivation and how to find motivated people. You will learn how to find and negotiate with motivated sellers and motivated buyers.

Hopefully, you find the information in this book useful. So let's get you started the right way.

Why I Wrote This Book

I have been involved in Lease Options for over seven years now. I have made a lot of mistakes and lost a lot of money using this investment strategy. But after I figured out what I was doing wrong, I made lots more money using this strategy.

What I have found, too, is that there are a lot of preconceived ideas about how to do a Lease Option transaction. This idea usually comes from "so-called" experts who have done less than ten transactions and who are teaching this strategy.

I was giving a workshop one year, and it became apparent to me, listening to the attendees, that Lease Options is a perfect strategy for people who want to get started in Real Estate Investing. What also became evident to me is that a lot of people are making a lot of mistakes doing them. Some mistakes are the same ones that I have made. Some were brand new to me. The other thing that became obvious to me is that people could have avoided a lot of those mistakes if they had just had more information. Information from someone that knows how to make money in Lease Options and someone who knows what it's like to make mistakes and lose money.

I wrote this book hoping that it will help you avoid at least one costly mistake, and to provide you with a better opportunity to make more money.

What is a Lease Option Investment

A popular type of real estate investing strategy is what's known as "Lease Option" investing or "Rent to Own" investing. Both these terms are used interchangeably. For simplicity, I will refer to this strategy as "Lease Option" from now on.

A Lease Option investment strategy is an investment strategy where a person rents the property from you, with an option to buy the property sometime in the future. How it is structured is simple.

Either you acquire a property, or you already own a property that you want to convert into a Lease Option. For whatever reason, you decided that you don't want to rent out that property anymore, so you make it a Lease Option.

There are lots of motivating factors why an investor wants to be in a Lease Option investment and lots of motivating factors why a tenant wants to do a Lease Option. The basic premise is that you buy a property, or you already have a property. The renter moves in and rents that property from you for a specified lease amount. A portion of that lease payment may go towards their down payment, or may not, depending on how much deposit they have and how much down payment they are saving.

Usually, when the tenant moves in, they provide you with a nice upfront amount, referred to as an *option consideration*. You use that amount of money to secure their "option to purchase" that property sometime in the future.

The tenant rents the property from you for 3 to 5 years, depending on the terms of the agreement. There many different scenarios that you might put together for a Lease Option arrangement.

After the three years, the tenant would buy the property for the previously agreed to price. That price must be determined at the start of the agreement, so when it comes time to buy the property in three years, there is no dispute over what that price will be.

So, it all starts with the option consideration payment. The tenant then makes monthly payments where they may build up a credit. Then after the three years, they purchase the house. During the three years, the tenants are leasing with an option to buy the property, thus the term *Lease Option*.

Why would someone want to do a Lease Option?

The tenant has many motivators. The main one is that they can't get approved for a mortgage and they want to buy a house now. It's because they have bad credit or no down payment or both. Those reasons are usually a result of other things.

Maybe they lost their job, but now they have one. Perhaps they had a sickness or death in the family, but now they have recovered financially. Many different scenarios would determine why a tenant buyer wants to do a Lease Option.

As an investor, a Lease Option is an excellent moneymaker

1. You get the initial deposit (option consideration).
2. You get monthly positive cash flow. You can almost guarantee positive cash flow with these Lease Option deals because the tenant is usually paying all the costs plus a credit, as part of the monthly payment. For example, if your monthly payment is $1,500 to cover just the costs, and your actual lease payment is $2000, you are making $500 a month.
3. You get the back end profit. Let's say you bought the property for 300,000, and you sell it to your tenants for 330,000. The difference is $30,000.

4. While the tenants are renting, they are also paying down your mortgage principle

Lease Option is a win-win

1. It's a win for the tenant because they get the property that they want *now*. They get a forced savings program to save for their down payment, and you help them build their credit score.
2. It's a win for the investor because you now have an investment property that has very little maintenance associated with it. There are two or three income sources, and these deals are pretty much guaranteed to cash-flow.

Check out **WWW.JIMPELLERIN.COM** for more articles on Lease Options and Real Estate Investing.

Chapter 1. The Real Nothing Down Deal

In this first chapter, I want to talk a bit about why the Lease Option approach is a *nothing down* deal.

Years ago, we heard about how you could buy a property with nothing down. People were talking about doing vendor take-backs or getting people to loan them the down payment. It really wasn't "nothing down." Nothing down, in this case, meant that they were getting other people to help fund the down payment. It meant nothing was coming out of their own pocket.

For example, in the case of a vendor take-back, the vendor was holding a second mortgage for them as the down payment.

Most of those types of transactions are gone now. Banks want you to have a certain amount of equity in the purchase. A certain amount of *skin in the game*. These days, it's tough to get lenders to allow you to purchase without using any of your own money.

Another way to purchase "nothing down" is to go borrow money from friends, from your lines of credit, or from your credit cards. These *nothing down deals* weren't nothing down. You were actually borrowing the money from other sources.

*So, when they say "nothing down" it really **wasn't a nothing down deal.***

With Lease Options, there's a huge opportunity to buy a property or to control a property with nothing down. One way would be for you to partner with another investor.

You find someone who has the money to invest. You, as the Lease Option expert, would partner with this guy. He would go out and purchase the property, and you would manage that property for that person until the end of the deal.

You now have a controlling interest in that property. Maybe you are registered on the title, or perhaps you're not. It depends on how you structure the deal. But you now have another property in your portfolio that was purchased as part of your joint venture. And you put in none of your own money.

Another way to do Lease Options is through a *sandwich lease*. What that means is that you find a motivated seller who has a property they can't rent or sell.

Maybe this seller had to move or some other reason. Maybe they found another job, and they can't sell the property for whatever reason. They are just normal homeowners.

Another reason might be that there's no equity in the property, or maybe the Realtor was just really bad, and they weren't able to sell it in time.

Now the person is carrying two mortgages ... two house payments. They have this old property to pay, and they have their newly purchased property also to pay. Or maybe they are just renting, which is still another place that they must pay.

Maybe they did something really stupid, and they bought another house without selling their current home because the Realtor told them that they should be able to sell their current house fast.

The bottom line is that they are now carrying two homes. These people are very *motivated*.

In this case, what you could do is enter into an agreement with the owner. The owner could lease it to you with an option to buy. Then what you would do is rent it to somebody else, giving them an option to buy as well. You have now created what is called a sandwich lease. We'll cover that in a future section.

Another option is that the owner would sell the house to you for what they owe on the mortgage, and they would transfer the property title to you. The owner will continue to be on the mortgage, but the property title is transferred to you. This transaction means you are taking possession through *subject to* financing since the owner is still holding the mortgage. So, in essence, the owner is financing the property for you. This approach is still a legal transaction, and a lawyer must be involved. The owner is actually selling the home to you for nothing down.

These are the real "nothing down" deals.

So, you have a motivated seller that you can do a sandwich lease with, and you have investors who are financing other deals for you. You, as a lease option expert, should be able to do lots of deals like this <u>without using any of your own money.</u>

Even the *closing costs* are covered by your investor or by the tenant buyer.

This is why I call Lease Options the real nothing down deal.

1.1 Motivation - Why People Want to Do Lease Options

The key to Lease Option investing is motivation

In a Lease Option, we look for motivation in a couple of areas. I get asked all the time ... *"Why would people do a Lease Option?"* "*Why would someone be motivated to do a Lease Option?*"

First, let's start with the buyer, the *tenant buyer*.

The tenant buyer is motivated because they can't get qualified for a mortgage. They either have poor credit or not enough down payment or both. They went to the bank, or they went to a mortgage broker, and they can't get qualified for a traditional mortgage. They are looking for ways to purchase a home, or at least, for ways to get into a home that they want.

The number one reason why people want to become tenant buyers and want to get into a Lease Option is that they want a house NOW. They want to have a beautiful place for their family to live in. They are tired of renting. Maybe the townhouse that they are living in is too small, so they are looking for a bigger home or a home that is more suitable for their family.

THEY CAN'T PURCHASE BECAUSE THEY HAVE BRUISED CREDIT.

Maybe they've gone through a divorce or suffered a death in the family, or they lost their job. Whatever the reason, these people cannot buy a home. The banks won't approve their application. So, that's the motivation for a tenant buyer.

The other side of a transaction is looking for motivated sellers. And this is where it gets interesting. A lot of people don't understand why a seller would do a Lease Option.

The *motivated seller* is someone who has a home and wants to sell it but, for whatever reason, they can't sell it. They are very motivated. They are very motivated because they are now carrying this property, which they don't live in and can't afford to make the payments. They are looking for a way to get rid of that extra monthly payment.

There are many reasons why these sellers would be motivated. First, they may have bought another home, and now they are also carrying the costs for both homes. They listened to their Realtor who said that this was a good market and convinced them to buy this new house without selling their existing home first. They told them that *"You shouldn't have any problem selling your existing home."*

They didn't even make the purchase conditional upon selling their current home. Now they're carrying two houses, and they are very motivated.

The second reason why a seller would be motivated is that they had to move.

Maybe they had to move for a new job, or perhaps they had to go back home to spend time with their family because they had a parent that was sick. They had to uproot themselves and move back home. They are very motivated to sell.

Another reason why they can't sell is that the property is not worth what their current financing is, so they would have to come to the closing with cash. Their house is "underwater." This situation means that they owe more than their home is worth.

Another type of seller that can be really motivated is an **investor**.

I get these motivated investors all the time. They have bought an investment property because they thought they wanted to be a real estate investor. They find a tenant. The tenant moved out, so they found another tenant. But they had to spend $5,000 or $6,000 or $7000 to pay for the damage from the previous tenant. Then the new tenant leaves as well.

So, it's just a bad situation for that investor because they don't understand how to be an investor. They watched all the shows about buying properties, renting them out, and making lots of money. Not to say that you shouldn't be investing like that, but you must make sure that you do your due diligence. You must be prepared to be an investor. You need the right training. You need more experience. Maybe you need a mentor. Someone to help you get started in real estate investing.

Now, this doesn't happen to everyone, but a lot of investors have come to me saying that they are fed up and ask me to take their property. They are very motivated sellers.

We have motivated buyers, motivated sellers, and motivated investors.

Some people can't retire because they don't have any place to invest their money. They are looking for better returns on their investment. Sure, they can put it into stocks and bonds and earn 1% to 5%, but people can't retire on those types of returns. I have friends that make over $200K a year, they have a million dollars in the bank, and they can't retire because 4% of $1M is only $40K a year. And when you are making $200K a year, that's a considerable drop in income.

These investors have been in the stock market for several years. They have put their money into registered retired funds and have even tried guaranteed investment certificates. They have tried various ways to invest their money, but those investments didn't give them the return that they needed to retire.

They are very motivated to find a suitable investment. They are looking for opportunities where they can earn more money, so they come to me looking for any real estate investment opportunities.

Lease Option is a perfect tool for these people. The *motivated buyer* who can't get qualified; we can help them. The *motivated seller* who can't sell their home for whatever reason; we can help them. The *motivated investor* who can't retire because they have no place to invest their money; we can help them.

THE CRITICAL COMPONENT WHEN LOOKING AT LEASE OPTIONS IS MOTIVATION

1.2 HOW TO FINANCE YOUR LEASE OPTION

How do you finance a Lease Option anyway? How do you get money to get started in Lease Options?

That's the thing about Lease Option Investing. There is no need to get financing.

There are three types of Lease Options, and none of them require your own money, which is why Lease Option investing is the real nothing down deal.

The first two ways that you can do a Lease Option is by finding property from an existing owner. That means going to the motivated seller or going to the motivated investor or going to the person that owns the property and negotiating with them to sign over their property. When you work with these owners, there's a couple of things you can do.

First, you can get the owner to lease the property to you. Second, you get them to transfer the title. Both approaches require no money out of your pocket. You don't have to finance it. You have an arrangement where you are taking over the existing mortgage, or you have an agreement that you are going to lease it from them.

There's a couple of ways to set that up, and we will go into that a little later. To be able to start a Lease Option arrangement, you don't have to put any money down, and there is no financing required.

If the owner is looking for a deposit before they will do the transaction, you can always get that deposit from your tenant buyer. There's still no financing required. You don't have to go to the bank or a lender to get a mortgage to purchase this Lease Option.

The third way you can set up a Lease Option arrangement is by using an investor to purchase the property.

The way this works is that we find a motivated buyer who can't get qualified and can't purchase a home. We show them a couple of our homes that we have acquired from motivated sellers. If they are not interested in any of those, we start shopping around until they find the house they want. Then we bring in an investor to purchase that home.

My arrangement with the investors is that they put up the money to cover all the costs. They put up the down payment, which is usually 20%. Most banks and lenders require a minimum of 20% down. The investor also pays for all the closing costs. That's often another 2%. For example, on a $300,000 home, the total investment required by the investor would probably be about $66,000.

Make sure that you have a *Joint Venture Agreement* in place that adequately specifies that *you* will be doing all the management work. You will find a tenant, find a property, and manage the property. What I do is I also guarantee the rents and cover any problems that we have with that tenant. In exchange, the investor puts up all the money. Again, there is no financing required by you. You would still have to get that investor qualified at the bank, but that's the extent of *your involvement* in the funding.

In summary, those are the three ways to enter into a Lease Option:

1. Find a motivated seller and enter into a sandwich lease arrangement with them.
2. Find a motivated seller and get them to transfer the property to you.
3. Find a Joint Venture Partner to purchase the property.

When arranging a Lease Option investment, you don't ever have to get financing. If you were to buy properties using money out of your pocket, you wouldn't be able to do that for very long. Because even if you had lots of money for the down payments, the banks would only lend you so much money. After a while, they won't want to give you anymore.

From a financing perspective, you don't ever have to finance your Lease Option investment if done correctly. Nor should you ever want to.

1.3 What is Your Role?

What exactly is your role in a Lease Option investment? As the expert, you are the person that will facilitate or "broker" the arrangement between the *motivated seller* and the *tenant buyer*. Why would a buyer or seller work with you anyway? Well, not many people know about Lease Options. Sure, they've heard the expression of rent to own, and they sort of know how it works.

Some people will even try to implement a Lease Option on their own property, but they may not have the right contracts. Maybe they don't understand the credits and the amounts they need to charge. Perhaps they don't know what the future purchase price should be.

Lease Options is all about putting somebody in a home where they are going to purchase it sometime in the future at a prearranged price. Well, if that price is not realistic and is not achievable, then that's a problem.

There's a lot of people out there trying to do Lease Options on their own, and for that reason, Lease Options have gotten a bad name. Some people are saying that Lease Options is a rip-off because the tenant is paying too much for the property. These naysayers don't understand what the benefits are to the tenant buyer.

From a tenant buyer's perspective, the main benefit that I have already mentioned is that they are getting into the property right away. They also have a more beautiful home than they would have without our help.

Why would they come to us? Because they need our help. They are looking for somebody to help them get a house. This help is similar to why people would go to Real Estate agents rather than just selling their property themselves.

People always look to other people to provide services for them. The service you are providing a tenant buyer is that you will find a home for them.

And why would a seller come to you? For the same general reasons. They are motivated, and they have run out of options. They can't get their home sold. Their Realtor can't get a high enough price because there's not enough equity in the house.

Again, it's all about motivation, motivation for the seller, and motivation for the buyer. So, they come to you looking for a solution.

Why do people go to a Realtor to help them sell their home? Why don't they sell their home on their own? Because they will probably sell it for the wrong price. It will either be overpriced or underpriced. Its either going to sit on the market for too long or it's going to sell too soon.

You want to use people with **experience.** When trying to convince tenant buyers, investors, and sellers to come to you, one of the main reasons you will highlight is that you have experience. You know how to do a Lease Option.

When I first started doing Lease Options, I made a lot of mistakes. I would never do a Lease Option the way I did years ago. I would never put that kind of transaction in place today.

There are some risks associated with doing Lease Options. People don't understand what those risks are. They could get into trouble with the purchase price. Are they charging enough? What about credits? How do you represent credits to the bank when the tenant goes to buy in three years? Tenant buyers are going to have a hard time getting qualified for a mortgage if they didn't do what they are supposed to do at the start of the agreement.

It's your job to make sure the tenant buyers, the sellers, and the investors understand the value that you're providing to them.

It all comes down to excellent marketing and explaining the benefits to your prospective clients.

Check out **WWW.JIMPELLERIN.COM** for more articles on Lease Options and Real Estate Investing.

CHAPTER 2. THE DIFFERENT TYPES OF LEASE OPTIONS

In this section, we are going to cover the different types of Lease Options.

1. PROPERTY-FIRST LEASE OPTION

A <u>Property-first Lease Option</u> is when you have a property, and you are trying to find a tenant buyer for it. There are many reasons why you would have a property first.

Maybe you have an investor who owns a property and wants to get rid of it. This investor is motivated. Perhaps you have a regular property owner who is trying to get rid of their property. This owner is motivated. Maybe you have an owner who is in a bad financial situation and is deciding to refinance their home to pay off their debt, but the banks won't let them. We could convert the owner into a Lease Option tenant buyer by buying their house. I call this a tenant-owned property.

A tenant-owned property is still just a seller, but this seller is going to become your tenant once they sell the property to an investor. That's what I call a **Lease-Buy-Back,** which is just another variation of the property-first Lease Option.

The owners have gotten themselves into a financial situation and can't get out of it. We must bring in an investor to purchase the property from the owner. The owner stays in the house and leases it back from us, thus becoming a tenant buyer. They enter into a Lease Option agreement.

In summary, there are three types of property-first Lease Options: the seller-owned, the investor-owned, and the tenant-owned.

Another property-first Lease Option would be if you went out and bought a property yourself because you thought it was a good investment and because it was a good deal.

2. Tenant-first Lease Option

The next type of Lease Option is a "tenant-first" Lease Option. This is where you go out and find someone who can't qualify for a mortgage but wants to buy a house. They found you as a result of your various advertising efforts. I also get a lot of my tenant buyer leads from my mortgage brokers because they have people who were looking to get a mortgage, but couldn't qualify them.

When we find a potential tenant buyer, the first thing we do is try to put them in one of the properties we already have in our listings. If they don't like any properties we already have, we go out, and we try to find a property from a motivated seller. It's relatively easy to pair up a motivated tenant buyer with a motivated seller.

Another way of finding a property in a tenant-first strategy is to purchase a property for them. As mentioned, the way we do that is through an investor or by purchasing it ourselves. Purchasing a property would be our last course of action. I would probably assign the deal to another Lease Option expert before I would purchase a property myself.

3. Sandwich Lease Option

The third type of Lease Option is what is commonly known as a Sandwich Lease Option. This is where we lease a property from a motivated seller, and then we sublet it to a tenant buyer. We sandwich ourselves in the middle of the deal. Really, it's just another variation of the property-first strategy.

In the following sections, we will cover these three types of Lease Options in more detail

2.1 Property-First Lease Option

A property-first Lease Option is when we have a property, and we are trying to find a tenant buyer to put in that property. The reason we would have a property-first is:

1. **Seller owned.** A motivated seller has a house that they haven't been able to sell. They had to move for a new job, or they purchased another home or many other reasons. They are motivated because they now have two mortgage payments, and they can no longer afford these payments. They are *very motivated* to sell.

2. **Investor owned.** An investor owns an investment property, and they are having a hard time managing the property. They have had bad tenants, and they are just fed up with being a landlord. They want out! *"Just take my property."* They are *very motivated*.

3. **Tenant owned.** A tenant owned property is where the owner has run up a bunch of bad credit and can no longer afford all their monthly expenses. Their housing expenses, their credit cards, and all those expenses that make up their monthly payments have gotten out of control. They must sell their home or lose it. They are usually close to foreclosure. They are very desperate, but they do not want to move. They like the neighborhood; their kids are enrolled in school there. So, we bring in an

investor, and we purchase the property from the existing owner, and the owner then becomes the tenant.

4. **Company Purchase.** I like a property, and I go out and purchase that property at a much-reduced price.

Now that we have the property, we have to find a tenant buyer. We must make sure that we market that property appropriately to the right target market. You will want to use many different marketing channels such as online classifieds, listing sites, social media, YouTube, etc. We must find a tenant for that property reasonably quick, or we may lose the opportunity.

You also want to be doing ongoing marketing to build up a database of tenant buyers. While it may be called property-first, it may be that you already have lots of potential tenant buyers that you are working with who are interested in a Lease Option.

Again, a Property-First Lease Option is when you have the property, and you are trying to find a tenant buyer for that property.

2.2 Tenant-First Lease Options

Some people would argue that Tenant-First Lease Options are much easier to do. My experience is that they are more challenging to do. First, you have to find the tenant buyer, you have to qualify that person, and then you have to find a property that they like. Next you have to purchase that property or convince a motivated seller to do a Lease Option with you.

The first thing we do when looking for tenant buyers is we advertise on different channels. We advertise on online classified ads, online 'For Sale by Owner' sites, on Twitter, on Facebook, on YouTube, etc. The other place where we find tenant buyers is through mortgage brokers and Realtors.

Potential tenant buyers are people that are trying to purchase a home, and when they apply for a mortgage discover that they can't get qualified. So now they are stuck. The purchasers are all excited because they thought they were going to purchase this property, and now they find out they can't. This is where we come in.

What we do in this case is we bring in an investor and buy that property for them. We work out a Lease Option arrangement whereby we lease the property back to people who couldn't qualify. It's not always the case that we have investors available. In that situation, we have to go searching for the right investor.

There are several things we do to find a qualified tenant buyer for a Lease Option.

First, we run our marketing to try and locate a tenant buyer. Then we do some pre-qualifying upfront. That usually means asking for a down payment and finding out what their income is. We need to know how much money they make so that when we go out looking for properties, we can find a property that is in their price range.

There have been many times where we have shopped around for a property with the tenant buyer, and then find out they don't have the deposit they said they had. There have been a few occasions where these people said they had their minimum deposit, which was $10,000, and we go out shopping with them, and it turns out they didn't have the $10,000. Then they ask us if we have some program where they could pay for their deposit in installments. I have tried doing installment plans in the past, and I have gotten burnt just about every time. I will never do that again.

You must make sure that you pre-qualify the tenant buyer before you go shopping for houses with them. When we look at their income, we also look at the Gross Debt Service (GDS) ratio and the

Total Debt Service (TDS) ratio to determine how much of a home that they can afford.

The GDS and TDS are calculations that help determine how much lease payment they can afford based on their income and debt (e.g., credit cards, car payments, etc.).

The tenant-first Lease Option strategy is about trying to find a qualified tenant that meets our criteria. A qualified tenant buyer means that they have the deposit and that they have enough income to cover their debt and rent to own payments.

Since the banks didn't approve these prospects, their credit score will be bad, or they didn't have enough down payment or both. We understand this when going into the deal. That's the nature of the Lease Option business. We know they are not the perfect loan candidates; otherwise, they wouldn't be coming to us.

Now that we have the tenant buyer, the next step is to go looking for a property for them. The first thing we try to do is show them one of the properties that we have available from motivated sellers or motivated investors.

If they don't like any of these, then we go out, and we look for other properties from other motivated sellers. Finally, if that doesn't work, then we look for investors to buy a property that meets the tenant buyer's specific needs.

Once we acquire a property, we put the contracts in place. There is no difference between the contracts that we use with the tenant-first arrangement and the contracts that we use for the property-first arrangement. It's the upfront work that we must do that is different between these two types of Lease Option strategies.

2.3 Sandwich Lease Option

A Sandwich Lease Option is where you, as the Lease Option broker, are sandwiched between the homeowner and the tenant buyer.

What that means is there is a contractual relationship between you and the seller as well as between you and the buyer. There are two contracts. There is a *Lease Agreement* and an *Option Agreement* between you and the seller.

The *Lease Agreement* between you and the seller would determine the lease payment to the seller, the term of the lease, and the responsibilities of each party.

So, for example, let's say your agreement with the seller is for $1,000 a month. You are leasing the property from the seller for $1,000 a month for three years, and you will take care of all maintenance and repairs.

Next, there is an *Option Agreement* between you and the seller that would determine the option price, the term of the agreement, and how the credits are to be applied.

For example, let's say that you have the right to purchase that property from the seller for $200,000. You would have an *Option Agreement* with the seller for $200,000, with $300 a month credits applied toward the down payment.

You have similar agreements with the tenant buyer. You have a *Lease Agreement* with the tenant buyer but for a higher amount. You *always* want to make sure that the amount that you are charging the tenant buyer is higher than what you must pay the seller. Otherwise, you will have a negative cash flow.

In this same example, let's say that you have an arrangement with the tenant buyer that you're going to collect from them $1,200 a month. That means you would have a $200 spread between what you are charging the tenant buyer and what you're paying the seller. That positive cash flow is essential in real estate investing. It's especially important when you're doing Lease Options.

The other contract that you have with the tenant buyer is the *Option Agreement*, which specifies that the tenant buyer has the right to buy the property from you for a higher amount. In this case, let's say that amount is 220,000. If you recall, you have the right to purchase the property from the current owner for $200,000. And since the tenant buyer has the right to buy the property from you for $220,000, that's a $20,000 profit spread.

So, you sandwich yourself in the middle of this whole lease option process, thus the name, "Sandwich Lease Option." It's a lot more complicated when it comes time for closing because now you have four contracts. The bank doesn't want to see all these contracts. They only want to see the *Agreement of Purchase and Sale* between the two parties: the seller and the buyer.

To finalize a Sandwich Lease Option, you would have to assign the contracts. Make sure the people you assign the contracts to know how to execute them at the end of the term.

So, at the end of the term, you can either assign your *Option Agreement* that you have with the tenant buyer to the seller, and they can execute it that way. Or you can even assign the *Option Agreement* you have with the seller to the tenant buyer. An assignment is very complicated, and I won't go into all the details here. A good lawyer will need to be involved. Just keep in mind that you are sandwiched between the two parties.

Another way you arrange this is to have a *Joint Venture Agreement* or a *Property Management Agreement* with the owner, and they have the *Option Agreement* directly with the tenant buyer. This arrangement avoids the issue of the tenant having an *Option Agreement* with you when you don't own the property. Optioning out a property that you don't own has become a legal issue with some of the transactions I have seen.

Check out **WWW.JIMPELLERIN.COM** for more articles on Lease Options and Real Estate Investing.

Chapter 3. Acquiring a Property

In this chapter, we will talk about how to acquire a property for your Lease Option deals.

When we started, we spoke about Lease Option investing being the real "nothing down" investment strategy. A lot of people who get into real estate think they have to spend a lot of money to get started, or they believe that they can't afford to get into real estate investing.

The difference between Lease Option or nothing down investing, and the other types of creative real estate investing, is that you don't need any of your own money to get started in Lease Option investing. All you need is drive and determination.

The funny thing is that drive and determination stops a lot of people because they must have a lot of motivation to want to succeed. They must have the *want* and the *desire* to go out and meet with people and talk to people to make things happen.

As discussed, there are four ways to acquire Lease Option properties.

1. The first way is by getting properties from a *motivated seller*.

2. The second way is by getting properties from a *motivated investor*. These are investors who have dealt with bad tenants and are very motivated. I have one investor who buys properties specifically to put into my Lease Option program. He does not want to manage it. He's motivated because he wants to start making money. This investor buys them pre-construction. He makes his $20,000 - $30,000 through a pre-construction deal, and then he hands them over to me. He doesn't want to have anything to do with the management of the property. As a result, we split the profit on a joint venture arrangement.

3. The third way to find porperties is through *motivated tenants*. These are people that currently own their own homes, but they have exceeded their ability to pay their ongoing monthly expenses. They sell the property to one of our investors, and we rent it back to them in a Lease Option arrangement.

4. The fourth way to acquire properties is through an *investor*. We have a motivated tenant buyer who has not been able to qualify for a mortgage. We bring in an

investor, and they purchase the property for the tenant buyer.

The first three options above are for properties from motivated owners. The last option is for a normal listed property or what I call a *Purchase Lease Option*. This last option is still a tenant-first Lease Option.

In the next sections, we will expand on all four ways to acquire Lease Option properties using these methods.

3.1 HOW TO ACQUIRE A LEASE OPTION PROPERTY FROM A MOTIVATED SELLER

The first and easiest way to acquire a Lease Option property is through a *motivated seller*. In earlier sections, we went through some reasons why a seller might be motivated. Maybe they lost their job and had to leave town. Now they have this mortgage payment, and they can't continue to make this additional payment for a property they are not living in. They are very motivated.

There are several ways to find these motivated sellers. A lot of times, you will see advertisements in either the *"For Sale by Owners"* ads or in the MLS listings that say right in the ad *"motivated seller."*

A trick that I use to determine if a seller is motivated is that I look in the online classified sites such as Craigslist or Kijiji. If there is a property listed both *For Rent* and *For Sale*, then you know you have a very motivated seller. That person is trying to get rid of that property any way they can.

What you should do to acquire this property is to contact them directly. You can contact the sellers yourself, or you can have somebody prequalify these sellers for you. There's only one question that you must ask these motivated sellers. *"If I could take over your property today and start covering all your monthly payments, would you continue to hold the mortgage?"* And if they say yes, then you know you have a very motivated seller. What that means is that you can do 1 of 2 things with this seller's property.

You can either get them to Lease Option the property to you, and since this is a book on Lease Options, that's the method that we will cover in more detail.

Or you can get them to transfer title to you, which I covered earlier and is called "subject to" financing. Keep in mind that there is a clause in most mortgage documents known as the "due on sale" clause.

Because of this clause, some people will say that it is illegal for someone to transfer title and still stay as the mortgage. That's not true. You can absolutely transfer the title, and it is legal.

It's not illegal, but the clause does say that if you do transfer the title, the mortgage that is currently on a property is due on sale. However, as long as you keep making those payments, the lender probably won't bother you. They may be interested or concerned about why the payments are now coming from a different person, but as long as you pay the mortgage, it's usually not a problem. I have done several of these transfers, and it's never been a issue. I tell the bank that I am the property manager looking after the property for the current owner and that the payments are coming out of this bank account. In those cases, I usually have a *Property Management Agreement* in place anyway.

In summary, the way you acquire a property from a motivated seller is you Lease Option it from them, or you transfer the title from the owner. Transferring a title is a *legal* transaction, and your lawyer will have to handle the transaction. There are costs associated with this transaction, but you can even get the owner to pay that cost, so there's no money coming out of your pocket.

So that's the easiest way to find motivated sellers.

When you contact sellers and ask them if they want to transfer the title into your name, and they say *no*, you know they're not that motivated. And you move on to the next prospect.

As mentioned, you can find motivated sellers in several ways.

Another way is you can talk to Realtors. Realtors aren't necessarily motivated to do this for you unless you can figure out a way to compensate them. Usually, you can pay them a referral fee using the money that you will get from your tenant buyer's deposit.

When you acquire a property from a motivated seller, make sure that you put in the agreement that you have 30 days or more to market the property, before you take control of the property.

So that's how you acquire a Lease Option property from a motivated seller.

3.2 How to Acquire a Lease Option Property from an Investor

Next, we are going to cover how to acquire a Lease Option property from an investor.

Believe it or not, this is probably the easiest way to acquire a Lease Option property.

Number one, it's easier to convince an investor to become a Lease Option investor because they are already an investor. It's just that they haven't been successful at being a *landlord*.

Earlier, we talked about why an investor is already a motivated Lease Option owner. It's because they weren't very good at being a rental investor. They had a string of bad luck with tenants, and they weren't very good at being a property manager. They didn't know how to qualify the tenants properly, and their tenants destroyed the property. So, they are an investor that wants to continue being an investor, but they are just changing their strategy a bit. They are going from being a hands-on investor to a very hands-off investor.

I have several investors like this. And believe me, once you find one of these investors and they have a lot of properties, this is a beautiful thing. I acquired ten properties from one of these investors.

You may also find some investors that are further along in their investment career. Maybe they were an investor for twenty years, and they are just tired of it now, so they want to get out of investing. But rather than dump the property and cash out, they know about Lease Options, so they look at it as alternative.

The contracts that you use for an investor will be the same contracts that you used for a motivated seller. You have the same arrangement with an investor that you have with a regular seller.

First, you look at what the value of the house is. How much do they owe? Keep in mind, an investor is going to be more knowledgeable than a regular seller. They may not be as willing to give up the property for what they owe. They may want a little bit more money. You must check the market to decide if what they are asking for fits into your strategy, and that you would be able to sell the property for that price.

Most investors would not want to hand over the title to you and do seller financing because they are more experienced. Instead, you might be able to do a Lease Option with the investor and sublet it to a tenant buyer.

It still comes down to how motivated the investor is. If they have just been through a string of bad luck with their tenants, the chances are that they are very motivated, and they are very interested in transferring the title to you.

When I first started doing these transactions years ago, I was in a hurry to try to get a deal done. I found that any deals I did where the parties weren't that motivated, turned out to be bad deals.

The underlying theme here is you're always looking for motivation. Real motivation! Not just someone saying, *"well, I thought about it, and maybe I'll do it."* If that's the situation, you don't want to enter into a transaction with those people because they haven't made up their minds about doing this.

So, the investor could transfer the title to you, or they could lease option the property to you. You would then do a lease option with the tenant buyer. You make money on the spread between your deal with the seller, and your deal with the buyer.

For example, let's say that you're paying the investor $1,000 a month with an option to buy it for $200,000, and you're charging the tenant $1,200 a month with an option for them to purchase from you for $220,000.

The arrangement you had with an investor would be very similar to what you would have with a motivated seller. It's just a little different situation because they already are investors, and you don't have to teach them to be an investor.

Investors are probably more willing to enter into this type of agreement than a regular seller would because a regular seller may need to sell to buy another property.

3.3 How to Acquire a Lease Option Property from a Future Tenant?

Next, I want to cover how to acquire a Lease Option property from a future tenant.

Another name for this is a *"Lease-Buy-Back."* With a lease-buy-back, we are looking for homeowners who are having a hard time making ends meet. I get calls all the time from mortgage brokers saying, *"Listen, I've got Bill in here, and he's having a hard time financially. He has run up a lot of debt, including lots of credit cards. He's got a second mortgage on the house, and he needs help to be able to pay off all these bills. Can you help?"*

By the time I get this call, the monthly debt obligations that were once $1,500 are sometimes almost $3,000. Now this person can't keep up with the monthly payments. He goes to the mortgage broker because he is trying to refinance his home.

Unfortunately, the mortgage broker can't do anything because there is not enough equity in the home, or the client's credit is damaged so much that he can't get approved for refinancing. Chances are he may even lose the house if the situation is that bad. He may have already missed too many payments.

What the lease-buy-back can do is bring relief to the current owner by buying the property from him, paying off all his debt from the proceeds of the sale, and renting the property back to him in a Lease Option arrangement.

What we can do in this situation is we can bring in an investor to purchase this property from the current owner. Then we lease it back to the owner in a Lease Option arrangement, where the owner now becomes the tenant buyer.

A lease-buy-back is no different from finding a tenant buyer, bringing in an investor, going out looking for a property, and then leasing the property to them. The only difference here is that we already know what the property is, so in a sense, it's a property-first type of transaction. But we also have a tenant, and all we have to do in this case is find an investor. So, it's a little bit different. It's not as challenging since we have the property and the tenant, and all we have to do is find the investor. Here's how it works.

First, we find an investor. Then we purchase the property from the current owner. The owner now becomes a tenant buyer and enters into a Lease Option agreement with the investor or with us. We execute all the standard contracts.

Now there are a couple of tricks that you can use when doing a lease-buy-back. First, you must make sure there's enough equity in the property to pay off all the debts that the owner is currently carrying. You want to make sure that the monthly payments are reduced to a more manageable level.

For example, let's say his property is worth $340,000 and that he owes about $250,000 on his mortgage, but he has another $50,000 worth of bills that he must pay off. What we would do is we would purchase the property from him for an agreed-to price.

Maybe that price is less than the $340,000 because we want to keep some equity in there for the back end, for when the owner repurchases it from us (that's another trick).

So, let's say we purchased the property from them for only $330,000. So now we have $30,000 of equity left that we would keep as the down payment for the eventual buy-back purchase in 3 years.

So, we are buying the house for $330,000. We are keeping $30,000 of it for the option payment. We are paying off $50,000 worth of bad debt that he accumulated, and we are paying off his existing mortgage of $250,000. The owner doesn't get any cash from the sale of their house, but they get all their debt cleared up. They also get to stay in their home, and they now have a lower overall monthly payment — not a bad situation for the owner.

We set up the Lease Option arrangement for whatever term we think is necessary — usually two or three years. We have an agreed price that they would purchase the property for in the future. That future price may be anywhere from $340,000 to $350,000 or even $360,000; whatever we feel that amount has to be for us to be able to make a reasonable profit on that transaction, just like any other Lease Option agreement.

That concludes the section on how to do a Lease Option transaction with the current owner who is becoming a tenant, which we also call a Lease-Buy-Back.

3.4 How to Acquire a Lease Option Property Using a Joint Venture Investor

Another way we acquire a Lease Option property is by using a Joint Venture Investor.

There are a couple of situations where we would use a Joint Venture Investor to acquire a Lease Option property. The first situation is when we have a new tenant buyer, and we need to buy a property. If you recall, this is the tenant-first strategy. We bring the investor in only after we have exhausted all other options and can't find the tenant a property from a motivated seller. We will then get an investor to purchase the property for the tenant.

The other situation where we use a Joint Venture Investor is for a tenant-owned property, where the owner is going to become a tenant. As mentioned, this is what we refer to as a Lease-Buy-Back arrangement.

Acquiring properties using Joint Venture Investors is very similar to when we are getting properties from motivated sellers. The only difference is the Joint Venture Investor is about to become the seller. And the big difference is that we must purchase the property. So, there is additional work upfront and there are other costs that this investor has to incur.

For example, if we were buying a property for $300,000 and the investor is required to put 20% down and pay closing costs of 2%, then the investor would have to invest $66,000.

I have to work with these investors to make sure that there is a reasonable rate of return built into these deals for the investor.

The investor makes money in a few ways.

Money is made in a Lease Option investment through the monthly cash flow, the principal paydown, and the sale price minus the purchase price. We have to make sure that the investor's profit is being taken care of by playing with those different areas of profit to ensure the investor gets a good rate of return.

What I also do for both the Joint Venture Investors and the motivated sellers, is guarantee the rent payments to them. So, if the tenant buyer doesn't pay me, I still pay the owners. Covering the rents helps reduce the sellers' risk and helps to convince them to do the deal.

Keep in mind that some of these sellers are about to become investors and they never planned on being investors. However, if a Joint Venture Investor becomes an investor, it's because they have made a conscious decision to do so.

The investors that I deal with are looking to be hands-off. They don't want anything to do with property management, tenants and they don't want to have lost rents.

As mentioned, I guarantee the rents for the investors during the life of the project, which is usually three years. Most of our lease option programs are for three years.

The other thing that I do is deal with all issues related to the tenants. For example, if the tenants are causing a lot of problems, we may even evict them. These investors don't want to be involved in the management of the tenants or property.

In summary, using Joint Venture Investors is one way that we acquire Lease Option properties. But we only use Joint Venture Investors when we have to purchase the property, either from an existing homeowner (Lease-Buyback) or when we buy a home for a tenant that didn't like any of the units we already had. It's our last resort.

Check out **WWW.JIMPELLERIN.COM** for more articles on Lease Options and Real Estate Investing.

Chapter 4. Making Money With Lease Options

In this section, we will cover how you make money with Lease Options. There are three ways to make money with Lease Options. At the front end, in the middle and at the back end.

The Front End

At the front end, you make money through the tenant buyer deposit. This money is paid by the tenant buyer as an initial payment when they enter into a Lease Option arrangement. Some people refer to this deposit as an option consideration and shy away from calling it a deposit because of similar contract terminology that is used in contracts when purchasing a home. They believe there may be legal ramifications associated with calling it a deposit.

In my Lease Option deals, I call it a deposit or an option consideration, depending on the contracts. We will go into that in the other sections.

The Middle

The second way you make money is throughout the term of the contract. A contract can be 2-5 years, depending on how long you want to run that Lease Option agreement.

You have a specific amount of money that you must pay the owner of the property and a specific amount that you will be collecting from the tenant buyer. The difference between those amounts is cash flow.

Also, there may be an amount that you add to the monthly payment as profit. And why would you want to add money to the monthly payment? It's because you are trying to get a specific rate of return that your backend won't allow. We will go into more detail in the next sections.

THE BACKEND

The third way to make money in Lease Option investing is when you sell the property at the end of the term or when the option is exercised. The backend profit is the difference between what the initial price that the seller wanted for the property and what the tenant buyer pays for the property. For example, if the seller is selling the property at $300,000, and the tenant buyer is buying it at $320,000, the difference is $20,000.

You can make a lot of money with Lease Options if you structure the deal properly. I make anywhere from $20,000 to $50,000 per deal, depending on the agreement.

We will now cover these three ways in more detail in these next sections.

4.1 Front End - Tenant Buyer Deposit

The first way you make money in Lease Options is through something called the *option consideration*, which is the amount of cash that your tenant buyer is going to put down when they enter the program.

When you advertise a property looking for a tenant buyer, one of the things you must make sure of is that you specify that the tenant buyer must provide a deposit. The amount required for the deposit is much different than what you would expect from a standard renter. The renter may only have to come up with the first month's rent and perhaps the last month's rent or a security deposit. Even combined, this amount would be a lot less than what you want for your Lease Option deposit.

If you are using an Option Agreement, then this deposit is usually referred to as an *option consideration*. An option consideration gives the tenant buyer the option to purchase that property for a specific price. For example, let's say your house is worth $300,000 today, and you told them that you would sell it to them in three years for $330,000. If they are using a Lease Option structure, they have the option to purchase that house at that price of $330,000 by giving you what is called an *option consideration*. That option consideration should be an amount of money, anywhere from 5% or more. Some investors will require less, and some require more. I require a minimum of $10,000.

Now you probably think if these clients had $10,000, why can't they buy the property themselves? Well $10,000 towards a $330,000 home is not even 5%. Most banks are looking for at least 5% as a down payment. At least in my area, that's what they want. Also, lenders will consider the applicant's credit score when evaluating people for a mortgage loan.

You can treat the deposit as a fee paid directly to you, or you can apply the deposit towards the down payment and deduct it off their purchase price when it comes time for them to buy.

The other way we structure the deal is by using the funds as an actual *deposit* towards the down payment. It's a deposit if you are using an *Agreement of Purchase and Sale* in what's called a long close or a deferred close.

For example, if the tenant buyer is buying the property in 3 years for $330,000, the upfront money the tenant buyer gives you is considered a down payment.

You are still collecting the money the same way. It's just written up differently. Instead of an *option consideration*, it's now a down payment, and it shows on the purchase and sale agreement as a down payment.

In conclusion, there are several ways you can treat this upfront payment. Whether it's 100% refundable or whether you keep it as a fee. The point is you are still getting cash upfront. That cash contributes to the overall cash flow and the profit you are making.

4.2 Middle - Monthly Profit

The next way you make money in Lease Option investing is through the monthly profit.

How that works is that you have a specified amount of money that you must pay your seller and a specified amount that you will be collecting from the tenant buyer. The difference is cash flow and profit. You may not even be paying the seller any profit, but you are still responsible for paying that mortgage to the seller. The principle is still the same. You must cover all the costs for the seller.

The costs that you must cover as part of owning a property are made up of a few things. These things are commonly referred to as PITI (Principal, Interest, Taxes, and Insurance.)

Monthly Credit

PITI is the costs that are normally associated with owning any property. If we are working with a tenant buyer where we have a forced savings program in place, we add an amount in addition to the PITI, which is called a monthly credit amount. What that means is that, sometime in the future, when the tenant is going to purchase the property, we are going to credit them that amount of money.

For example, let's say our total PITI costs come to $1,500. And let's assume the tenant buyer gave us $10,000 as a deposit. And let's say they are buying a house for $300,000. If the down payment they will be required to save is 5%, that means they need $15,000 as a down payment. Since they have already given us $10,000, we must put together a savings program where they are providing an additional $5,000 over the three years.

Using rough calculations, if you spread that $5,000 over three years, they would pay an extra $150 per month. $150 a month is a total of $5,400. That $5,400 plus the initial $10,000 would come to

$15,400, which is a little more than the 5% required to purchase.

Now you have a positive cash flow since you are collecting $1,500, and you are receiving another $150 that you only have to credit in the backend. What you are doing is just pre-paying your profit from the deal. The good thing is that it is cash flow. In real estate investing, cash flow is KING.

Some people who I have talked to say, *"the property doesn't have to cash flow because I am basing my return on appreciation, and I'll make money when I sell it."* Well, you know what happened to house prices a few years ago. I wouldn't count on appreciation for my profit.

Management Fee

Another thing you can do is you can add an amount for a management fee.

For example, let's say you add another $250 of pure profit as a management fee. That means that you will get an additional profit of $250 a month spread over 36 months, which means you are making about $9,000 of extra profit in total.

Of course, some people will think that you are ripping off the tenant by charging them this management fee. Well, you are in business, and you want to make sure you make a minimum amount of profit on these deals.

Some of my investors will hold out and only make their profit in the backend when the tenant buyer buys the property in 3 years. As mentioned, that's a risky approach because you can't be sure what that property is going to be worth in 3 years.

I am running into that right now where we have an option price, and now the property isn't worth that amount. I'm stuck with having to figure out how to sell that property, and it's causing me some significant problems.

So back to our example. You are collecting $1,500 PITI plus $150 credit plus $250 profit for a total of $1,900 a month. And $400 of that is cash flow. Of that $400, $250 is pure profit, and another $150 is potential profit.

That's a perfect way to make a monthly profit that gives you excellent cash flow.

4.3 Back End – Selling

The third and final way you make money with Lease Options is in the backend when you sell the property.

When you purchase a property or when you acquired a property from a seller, there is a starting price that is established. It's usually based on the current market value.

For example, let's say that you negotiate with the seller that a reasonable price is $300,000. Or maybe, in the case of a *purchase* Lease Option, you paid $300,000 when you bought the property.

It's now three years later or 4 or 5 years later, and you are currently selling that property. And hopefully, you are selling it to the tenant buyer.

That tenant buyer has an option agreement to purchase at an already specified amount. That amount might be $330,000.

So, you purchased the property for $300,000, and you are now selling the property for $330,000. The price seems pretty good, right? You have made a $30,000 profit.

The other way in which money is made at the end of a transaction is through the principal paydown.

For example, in our $300,000 home, there might be an additional $10,000 of mortgage principal that was paid down over three years. The amount of principal paid down will depend on the starting mortgage amount, the mortgage interest rates, and the amortization period.

Who gets the benefit of the principal paydown will depend on how you set up the deal with the seller. If the arrangement is a purchase lease option, the seller may get the benefit from that principal paydown. Who gets the benefit of the principal paydown can be worked out as part of the negotiation with the seller? You would tell the seller that, as part of this arrangement, you would be paying down their mortgage for three years. Explain to them that they are making money on their investment. In this case, the seller would benefit from the principal paydown.

For example, if their property was worth $300,000 and maybe we would expect to pay down the mortgage by $10,000. That works out pretty good for the seller, assuming they had very little equity, which is usually the case for a motivated seller.

So, assuming they only had $30,000 of equity and now I am telling them we are going to be paying their principal down by $10,000 over three years. That is an excellent return on their investment (33%). That return is a perfect selling point when negotiating with the seller to stay on the mortgage and to do a Lease Option.

Don't forget that when it comes time for the tenant to buy in 3 years, you must make sure that you allow for the option credits and the deposit. If you recall in previous sections, we talked about the tenant putting down $10,000 as a deposit and the tenant also entering into a forced savings program where they are saving an additional amount, let's say $200 a month, towards their purchase.

The deposit and the savings will make up the down payment for when they go to purchase the property. In 3 years, if the tenant buyer is purchasing the property for $330,000, we have to make sure that they have accumulated $17,500 through the deposit and forced savings credits. These credits will reduce the profit that you get on the backend, but you receive the profit monthly as cash flow instead

The down payment will be made up of the deposit and the monthly forced savings payments. Don't get too excited thinking that you have made all this money upfront, in the sense that you made $10,000 as a deposit and the monthly savings plan payments. You still have to use this money as the down payment when the tenant buyer purchases the property. The $200 a month that you are collecting as the forced savings must be credited at the backend when the tenant buyer buys.

For example, if the original sale price was $300,000 and the future Option Price was $330,000, the profit you should receive is $30,000. But you have already been paid a portion of that profit when you collected the $10,000 deposit and another $200 a month as part of the forced savings monthly payment plan. The combined amount you are paid is $17,200, which will be applied to the down payment. The net proceeds you would receive from the sale would be $330,000 - $300,000 - $17,200 = $12,800.

That concludes our chapter on how to make money with Lease Options.

Check out **WWW.JIMPELLERIN.COM** for more articles on Lease Options and Real Estate Investing.

Chapter 5. Finding Tenant Buyers

In this section, we want to talk about how to find tenant buyers. Finding tenant buyers is not as hard as you might think. What we are looking for when we are looking for tenant buyers is somebody who has a good income, has bad credit and has the necessary deposit.

The situation with the tenant buyers is that they are not able to qualify for a mortgage, so they are looking for alternatives.

There are many ways to find tenant buyers.

You can advertise online, through social media, ask your friends, or work with professionals.

I have tried traditional marketing for a while, but it doesn't seem to be working anymore. I can't remember the last time I saw somebody with a physical newspaper. Most people are reading news online now.

When I refer to online advertising, I mean online advertising through various sites such as Craigslist, Kijiji, and various social media channels, such as Facebook, Twitter, and LinkedIn. You should also be looking at email campaigns and your website.

You will need to have a good website for people to check out who you are and what you do. You can use Facebook paid ads, and Google pay-per-click ads to drive traffic to your site or a landing page. All these things that I just listed are online advertising.

The type of advertising that you choose will depend on if you have a property or if you don't have a property. If you have a property, it's better. It's a lot easier to advertise a house looking for tenant buyers than if you didn't have one, and all you are doing is promoting your services, looking for tenant buyers.

Another way to find tenant buyers is through your relationships with professionals. If you are in the real estate investing business, you should already have relationships with mortgage brokers, Realtors, and other people in your local real estate investing group. They might have a motivated buyer come their way that they could refer to you.

In these next sections, we will go into more detail on how to find tenant buyers.

5.1 Advertising for Motivated Buyers

The first way to find tenant buyers is to advertise for them.

Websites and Flyers

Before you get into advertising and social media and all the different types of online lead generation techniques, you have to make sure that you have a landing page or a website where people can go to learn more about your business.

It doesn't have to be elaborate, but you do need a website. If you are running this as a business, you must have a place where people can go and read about you. Tenant buyers want to know a little bit about your program. There's a lot of information you can put on a site. You also have to make sure you have handouts when you go to meet potential customers.

A website and handouts are the basic prerequisites before you start advertising. People are going to want to see more information. They are going to want to know more about your program. Make sure that if you're looking for motivated buyers, sellers, and investors you have three different websites. You don't want your tenant buyers to know how much your investors are making. You should have three different sites, and you want to drive traffic to those sites in different ways.

OFFLINE ADVERTISING

As you may know, or as you might have guessed, traditional advertising has pretty much gone away. Not a lot of people are advertising in printed newspapers anymore.

I'm not sure if anybody even reads the printed newspaper anymore. A lot of people are reading the news online, usually on the online version of the printed newspaper.

Direct mail flyers might work if you target them properly.

For example, if you have a property in a specific neighborhood, you can send out a flyer to the neighboring community. The flyer would advertise the available home. It would stress the benefits, such as "no bank qualifying", and explain that the tenant could move into that properly fast. All they need is a small deposit to get started. So, targeting local areas with flyers might work.

Another place to try offline advertising is in the local newspapers that get sent out to people in a specific community. I've had some success running ads in these community papers. The fact that they still send these out and people read them means that they must still work.

You can even try local radio. Keep in mind that the radio is costly. For one month, I was paying anywhere from $3,000 to $5,000 for a very small number of 15-second time slots. Radio ads can be effective but very expensive.

ONLINE ADVERTISING

Online advertising is a whole different ball game.

Online advertising is all about using the *'For Sale by Owner'* (FSBO) sites and online classified ads sites.

For example, you have probably heard of Craigslist. In Canada, we have Kijiji. There are a few other sites, including eBay classifieds. I'm sure there are a lot more sites specific to your area. Your strategy changes depending on if you have a property or not.

FSBO sites are sites where people are posting their properties and looking for buyers, tenants, and even tenant buyers. Some sites will let you post your property as a Lease Option or a rent-to-own.

There may be a fair bit of competition on these sites, and some of the sites may charge you to advertise. While a lot of the online classified sites are free, they usually offer a paid option, which provides you with a lot more features. There are probably some local FSBO sites in your neighborhood that you might want to check out as well.

Another type of online advertising is using paid advertising. Google and many social media platforms offer PPC and paid advertising options.

Google AdWords and Facebook are the most popular paid advertising platforms. Google Ads are set up so you only have to pay whenever anyone clicks on your ad. You don't have to pay for impressions.

Those ads are presented to people on Google when they are performing a search. When the search results page is presented, the ads are shown at the top of the search results page.

Google ads are not as effective as they used to be. People are getting used to seeing those ads, and so they are not paying as much attention to them anymore.

People that are searching feel that companies that know what they are doing are probably in the center of the search results page, where the organic search results appear. As a result, most searchers would select one of those organic sites instead of the ad.

Most social media platforms have a form of paid advertising. For example, Facebook/Instagram, TikTok, Twitter and even YouTube has paid advertising.

With Facebook, you can target your ads more specifically. You can present Facebook users with a post, that is an ad. The ad could be showing a specific property that you are looking for a tenant buyer for. Facebook ads are an excellent way to drive traffic to find tenant buyers. Compared to Google Adwords, Facebook Ads are a lot less expensive.

You want to make sure you are measuring and tracking all your advertising and your advertising results. You want to know where your leads are coming from. You want to know what kind of conversions and opt-ins you are getting on your site.

Another thing you should be doing as part of your online marketing is capturing people's emails using an opt-in form and adding those emails to an autoresponder. An autoresponder is a useful tool that you can use to keep in touch with your prospects regularly. You can use an autoresponder to set up a drip campaign to send ongoing email messages to your prospects automatically.

And make sure that you measure everything. Make sure you understand where all the traffic is coming from.

So that concludes our section on advertising.

5.2 Using Social Media to Find Motivated Buyers

Another way to find tenant buyers is through social media.

Using Social media to find tenant buyers, is a very different approach. What you are trying to do with social media is to provide tenant buyers with useful information. Over time, you are building a relationship with these people.

The first thing you need to do to prepare for your social media activities is to set up a blog. I know that sounds strange. But what you are going to do is use your blog as the place where you want to direct everybody from your social media sites.

You will post Lease Option articles to your blog regularly. Your articles will describe how your readers can benefit from Lease Options. Your blog posts don't have to be that long. They can even be a video.

In your blog posts, you could talk a bit about the neighborhood that you are focusing on. You can post a new property that you have. You can write about a deal that just happened. You can write about how people are benefiting from Lease Options. You can write about current mortgage rates. You can write about the current economic situation.

These are all topics that are of interest to tenant buyers.

You can also write about credit, credit repair, the minimum credit required. You could write about Gross Debt Service (GDS) ratios and Total Debt Service (TDS) ratios. All the financing topics that tenant buyers might be interested in.

You could also record videos on YouTube and have your very own YouTube channel. YouTube is very popular. It is the second most popular search engine, next to Google. People are watching videos, and they might decide to search on how to buy a house or how to qualify for a house.

Here's the process I use. First, I record a video. Next, I transcribe that video. Then I take that content (video and transcription), and then I post it on my blog as an article. Then I post about the article on my social media channels with a pointer back to my blog. I can even run FB ads to the post.

All you have to do is create content and then tell people about that content.

The most popular social media platform is Facebook, and it's probably the one that tenant buyers are hanging out on the most. Instagram is also very popular and is owned by Facebook. And more recently, TikTok may be a platform to target.

You won't find as many tenant buyers on LinkedIn. LinkedIn is where you are more likely to find investors or sellers. People looking to purchase a home are probably hanging out on Facebook. Instagram and TikTok. Twitter might work, as well.

Every time you post an article on your website, you should post a link on Facebook, Instagram, TikTok, and Twitter. That blog post can be just text, or it can have a video with text.

Write a post saying something like, *"here is an interesting article I just wrote on how to repair your credit within six months"* or *"how to raise your credit score by a hundred points within six months."* The great thing about posting links on social media is that you don't have to be the author of that article. You can write the article yourself, or you can curate the content.

You can also go out and find other people's articles. You need to get their permission to post those articles on your website. Once you do, post a link to the articles on your social media sites. This will get your followers to come to your website/blog to read the article and learn more about you and your Lease Option program.

Your blog should be a component of your website. So, when they are on your blog, you're also exposing them to information about your program. That way, your visitors can read all about your Lease Option program. It's all about keeping your followers informed and about building a relationship with your followers. That's what social media is all about.

The other social media platform that you want to be active in is Twitter. For some reason, people like these short tweets. So, when you're creating content for your blog, you want to make sure that your titles are condensed enough so that it looks good on Twitter.

In summary, Facebook, Instagram, TikTok, and Twitter are the most popular social media platforms that you should focus on. Your YouTube channel can be used to host your videos.

Use paid social media ads to drive traffic to your site. You can also use Google ads to understand what keywords people are searching for. Once you have a list of keywords, you should be writing articles that are optimized for those keywords.

Search engine optimization around keywords is a whole different activity that I will cover in another book. For now, focus on putting out good content and linking to it from your social media platforms. This should get you lots of traffic without too much effort.

5.3 Use Professionals to Find Motivated Buyers

Another way of finding tenant buyers is through your relationships with industry professionals.

Let's start with Realtors. Realtors are always finding people that want to buy a home. But some buyers that come to realtors may not be preapproved, or worse, the Realtor didn't check to see if the buyer was pre-approved. The buyer and the Realtor go through the whole process of trying to purchase a home. Then they find out that the buyer can't qualify for a mortgage. The Realtor has to find a solution fast.

So, they come to us and say they are in the middle of a transaction and ask us for help. We bring an investor in, and that investor purchases the property.

Probably, the best professional group to find tenant buyers from is mortgage brokers. Mortgage brokers know their buyer's financial situation, and they know their ability to purchase a house and whether they can get a mortgage. Mortgage brokers get all the buyer's financial information, and they run a credit check. They can tell right away if these buyers can purchase a home or not.

Mortgage brokers can quickly determine if the buyer can qualify for a conventional mortgage or not. If they can't qualify, they can send them over to us.

If I get a referral from a Realtor, I will try to use the Realtor in the purchase transaction. If I have to purchase a home using an investor, I will use the Realtor that referred the buyer to me, especially if the Realtor is currently working with that buyer, and the buyer couldn't qualify. What we do is bring in the investor in place of the original buyer to purchase that specific property.

If I get a referral from a mortgage broker, we will send the investor over to that mortgage broker to get them approved for a mortgage. This is assuming the investor is okay with using this mortgage broker. Sometimes the investor may have their own banker or mortgage broker they deal with.

The other thing I could do for the mortgage broker is let them do the mortgage that the tenant would need in 3 years.

Other professionals you will use are other real estate investors. Investors are out there looking for deals and opportunities. They might have someone they were working with who was going to purchase a property that they had just finished doing a fixer-upper on. It turns out that the buyer couldn't get qualified and so the investor sends them to us to see if we can help.

Some real estate investors do *bird-dogging*. Bird-doggers can be out there working for you looking for deals for you. These people will want to meet with you to find out what you are looking for and to find out what types of transactions you do. They will want to know whether you are looking for investors or motivated sellers or tenant buyers. You would need to work out an agreement for how much you will pay your bird-dogger for a lead or a closing, depending on what they are doing for you.

Bird-dogger referral fees can be anywhere from $200-$500, depending on the type of referral you get. A referral fee could also be as high as $3,000 to $5,000, depending on how much work they will do for you.

I tend to pay people in the higher range because some of the people that are bringing referrals to me are coming to me with a signed *Lease Agreement* and a signed *Agreement of Purchase and Sale*, so the deal is pretty much done. All I have to do is sign it and take the deal and manage it for three years.

The other place where you might find motivated buyers is from people in similar industries. For example, people who are in the finance industry: bankers, financial planners, insurance agents, etc. These people meet potential tenant buyers all the time. They may have new clients that they can't help, or there may be people whom they have been dealing with, and these people have now come into some financial difficulties and need a solution.

Another group of professionals, whom you can get referrals from is credit counselors. Credit counselors meet people all the time who may be thinking of bankruptcy or a consumer proposal. Maybe we can help them by buying their home from them and refinancing it and making them a tenant buyer in a lease-buy-back situation.

The key here is to get out there and let people know what business you are in, and maybe they will work with you.

Chapter 6. Finding Motivated Sellers

In this section, I want to talk about how we find motivated sellers.

There is a big difference between looking for sellers and looking for tenant buyers. When looking for sellers, we must do our own search. With tenant buyers, they are searching for us, because we have homes.

The best places we go to look for sellers are the property listing sites, in MLS, and in any other site where sellers are listing a property, such as Craigslist. You will be looking for motivated sellers. A motivated seller will be obvious by how they are advertising. In some cases, they say that they are motivated.

Another place you can go to find motivated sellers is by talking directly to Realtors and mortgage brokers. Realtors and mortgage brokers are working with people who are buying and selling homes.

An excellent way to meet Realtors and mortgage brokers is by attending networking events. When you are at these events, and you are networking with people, make sure you tell them that you are a real estate investor and that you are looking for homes to acquire.

When looking for motivated sellers, you can also place your own ads. You can put ads on classified ad sites such as Kijiji, Craigslist, and other websites. You can put up bandit signs throughout the city. These are signs that are nailed or stapled to telephone or hydro poles or just stuck in the ground. They are usually put up late at night or early in the morning, which is why they are called *bandit* signs since this is when bandits are out and about. Now a lot of cities have cracked down on bandit signs and don't allow them. Still, some investors continue to use them with some success and without any problems.

Another place when you can look for motivated sellers is to advertise at another home that you are trying to sell.

In the following sections, we are going to address these different ways in which we can find motivated sellers and motivated investors.

6.1 Searching for Motivated Sellers

The first way we can find motivated sellers is to go out and search for them.

There are many places where you can search for potential, motivated sellers. You can start by searching the FSBO sites, Zillow, Trulia, the MLS sites, and any site that has houses for sale. Just go to Google and search *"homes for sale."* Some people are creative, so they will create their own sites to try and sell their homes that way.

The critical thing to realize when you are looking for motivated sellers is first to determine if they are, in fact, motivated.

One of the things you can do to find out if the seller is motivated is to read the "house for sale" ad.

The first thing you should be looking for is **when** was the ad posted. How long has it been on the market? If a property was only listed for one month, it's probably not going to be a good opportunity for you because the seller may not be that motivated. But maybe there are some words in the ad that shows that they are really motivated and that they must sell. But that's an exception.

Generally, the date when the ad was posted is definitely a good indicator of motivation. If the listing was posted 3 or 4 or 5 or even six months ago, the chances are that they are very motivated. Keep in mind that these sellers are probably inundated with a bunch of Realtors trying to get their listing, so these sellers may not be very receptive to you.

The best approach to use is to call these people up and find out what the situation is. You will have to talk to the sellers explaining what it is that you are trying to do. You explain to them that you would be taking over their payments and eliminating their problems. You will need to build a rapport with them.

So, the longer the seller has been trying to sell their house, the more motivated they are to enter into a *Lease Agreement* or to transfer their title over to you. They are feeling the pain of the monthly payment. For most people, a $1,000 to $1,500 extra monthly payment hurts; especially, if they had to carry it for 4 or 5, or 6 months.

The situation is usually that the owner has been carrying the payments for several months. The banks are calling them, and their creditors are calling them. These sellers are very interested in hearing about your program.

When we approach people, we tell them that, if they let us market their property, we could probably put somebody in their house in 30 to 60 days. Then we ask them if this is something that they would be interested in? Then we offer to take over their property for what they owe on it?

Motivated sellers are very interested in hearing what we have to say. They are tired of talking to their creditors looking for payments and hearing from Realtors looking for a listing.

Another thing you can do is outsource the finding of motivated sellers. By outsourcing, I mean, you can either hire somebody or get your assistant to do it for you. It's pretty straightforward.

You will need to put together a script that someone can use to gather some initial information. There are some key pieces of information you will want to get. For example, what is the asking price? How much do they owe on the property? What are their monthly payments? How far are they behind in their payments? Do they need to sell the property, or can you take over their mortgage payments if they stay on the mortgage?

Once you develop that script, all you have to do is give it to the person to whom you have outsourced this work. Whether it's your assistant or whether you hire someone specifically to do this for you. Fiverr is an excellent place to find someone to help you.

Another thing you can do to find sellers is to use *"bird-doggers."* Bird-doggers are people that are interested in finding opportunities for you in exchange for a referral fee. They will contact sellers for you once they know what you are looking for. Once they see that you're looking for houses for your Lease Option program and you have explained how your program works, these bird-doggers will get on the phone and start calling sellers for you.

Bird-doggers will generally be more expensive than an assistant. But, because they're more expensive, you will expect them to do a lot more. They won't just be cold calling to determine if these people are eligible for the program. They may be putting the whole deal together. They will be closing the deal and getting contracts signed off. Of course, it will depend on the arrangement you have with them.

Realize that when you start contacting sellers, you aren't going to find a house on your first call and maybe not on your second or third, or even your tenth call. You're probably looking at making between 20, or 30 calls before you find someone that might be interested in your program.

Like anything else, in sales, it's a *numbers* game. The more calls you make, the more deals you make. Make sure you make enough calls to get enough responses to be able to get a deal.

If you practice this approach every day, you should be finding at least 1 or 2 sellers a week that are interested in entering into your program and maybe even 3 or 4 of these a month.

So, in summary, the first way in which you can find motivated sellers is by searching on web sites and calling them.

6.2 Advertising for Motivated Sellers

Another way you can find motivated sellers is to advertise for them. By advertising, I mean placing ads in online classified ad services. For example, Craigslist and Kijiji (in Canada), are some other online classified ad services. You can also try many of the online for sale by owner sites.

The thing about advertising for motivated sellers is that there are not a lot of Sellers that are looking for your solution. There is no place where motivated sellers can go and say, *"how do I sell my house fast."* Most of the people who are in a difficult financial situation (motivated), and who are trying to sell their house, will be looking at selling in one of the following ways.

One way motivated sellers might be trying to sell their home is by selling it themselves because they can't wait any longer or because they can't afford a Realtor. They are advertising the property "For Sale by Owner" on the FSBO sites.

The other way they would try to sell is by using a Realtor. But sometimes that Realtor is not a viable option because the owner doesn't have enough equity in the home to even pay for that Realtor. So, maybe the owner is really stressed, and they are trying to save money, and things aren't moving fast enough.

The Realtor has had the property listed for one, two, or three months and the owner is fed up. A lot of times, the owners will place their own ads along with whatever advertising the Realtor is doing.

An excellent way to find motivated sellers is by running social media ads. You can advertise best using Facebook Ads. These ads can be targeted based on age, location, and even personal interests.

Another place to advertise online is Google AdWords. When using Google AdWords, make sure you use the right keywords. For example, in addition to *"we buy houses fast"* maybe you would look for *"credit problems"* or *"home equity loans."*

The key when advertising online for motivated sellers is to be creative. Make sure your ad headline is compelling, so motivated sellers can find you. Use the right keywords for your ads. Look for the right ad sections to place your ad.

Keep in mind that you may not be allowed to post an ad in the ad sections where you want to post an ad.

For example, one place you may want to post your ad is where people might be looking to sell their homes which is in the "Homes For Sale" section, which is where motivated sellers might be looking to see how other people are posting their ads. However, these online classified sites may not allow you to run an ad saying, *"Can't sell your house? Call us; we may be able to help you."* These sites won't allow you to run an ad like that because you're merely soliciting and not selling a house.

One section I advertise in Kijiji is the *"Real Estate Services"* section. However, there aren't a lot of people looking in this section.

Keep in mind that there are a lot of people advertising for the same thing that you are advertising for. You have to make your headlines stand out. You have to make your ads unique. You may even need to pay to promote these ads. Don't get caught looking like everybody else.

If you need to spend a little money to get your ads seen more, then don't be afraid to spend it. You will need to spend money on your Facebook ads, on your Google AdWords ads, and to promote your online classified ads.

Be smart about looking for motivated sellers. Make sure that you're not just saying you are *"looking for people who are motivated that can't make the payments so we can help."* Be more creative in the sense that you're looking for solutions for these motivated sellers' problems.

Focus on other keywords that you think motivated sellers might be searching on. This applies to all three of the ad types that I just mentioned: Facebook ads, Google ads, and online classified ads. Make sure that you are spending some money on your Facebook and Google ads. You want to get as much exposure as you can so that people can find you.

In summary, it's a lot harder to advertise looking for motivated sellers, than it is to go out and search the places where motivated sellers have properties listed for sale.

6.3 Networking for Motivated Sellers

The last way to find motivated sellers is by networking. By networking, I don't mean just going to parties and talking to people. I mean seeing and talking to the right people.

First of all, everyone you talk to should end up knowing the type of business you are in. And not just that you are in Real Estate investing. You need to be very specific about what you are doing.

Make sure people know that you are helping people who have financial problems and who can't meet their monthly payments on their homes. Specifically, you help those people solve their problems by taking over their monthly payments.

Some people know that what you do is called Lease Options or Rent to Own. Whatever the more common term that people are familiar with in your neighborhood, that's what you need to start using. Start explaining your program to them in that way.

For example, in one community I invest in, Lease Options is a very common term. Another city that I am active in has never heard of a Lease Option. Rent to Own is a term they know about and has been around for a long time.

Before you start networking, you need to come up with an elevator pitch, if that's what you want to call it. I hate that expression, but it's just a description of what it is that you do and how you want to describe it, so people understand.

Once you have your pitch, then you want to meet with people who might be interested in your services. You need to talk to professionals who deal with motivated sellers. One type of professional is people in the finance industry. You want to start a relationship with all the financial planners in your area.

You want to start a relationship with bankers. However, bankers might not be so keen on referring somebody to our program because they might not like some of our arrangements where we take over the property and transfer the deed while the owner stays on the title.

As long as these people are okay with the transfer, then maybe they will be okay with dealing with you. As long as the bank is making money, they may be happy.

When you take over someone's title, you are not doing anything illegal. The only thing that happens is that the due on sale clause may be activated. In all the deals I've done, the lender has never called the due on sale clause.

The other type of financial person that you want to network with is a mortgage broker or mortgage agent. Mortgage brokers get approached all the time by people with credit problems trying to refinance their homes. These people have run into real problems. Most of my refinance deals that are referred to me come from mortgage brokers.

The mortgage agent contacts me and tells me that they have clients who came to them looking for a second mortgage or looking to refinance, and they can't help them because their client doesn't have the credit. Their client is going to be bankrupt if someone doesn't help them.

We will look at the situation and present alternatives to their clients. One option is where I bring a third-party investor in to buy that home and lease it back to the owner. That's what we refer to as a lease-buy-back, which we already covered.

The other option for these people is they would hand over their house to us go and rent another house on their own. In this case, we would take over their monthly payments, if this makes sense for us to do so. In most cases, this is a much better situation for these people.

For example, let's say the owners are paying $2,000 a month for their mortgages. And let's say I can rent it out for $2,500. That's the type of deal I would be very interested in doing. For example, the owners would find another place to rent at a much lower monthly payment of $1,000 or $1,200 a month.

Networking is a fundamental way to find motivated sellers. Networking is essential, if people know what it is that you are doing.

Don't be shy about talking about real estate investing. People sometimes try to hide it from other people. They think people will think they are this big-shot real estate investor, and they will be treated differently, or people will talk to them differently or think they are a snob. Don't worry about that.

Make sure you are talking to people and that they understand what it is you do. Whenever I'm with people, they are always asking me, *"so how's the real estate business?"* Eventually, people will ask me what it is that I do. Sometimes I'll arrange to have lunch with them and explain what it is I do. Even if these people aren't interested because they aren't motivated, they could become an investor. Or maybe they have friends or family that are motivated. Or perhaps they know someone that might be interested in my service either as a motivated seller or as a motivated buyer.

In summary, make sure you're communicating your service effectively. Network with the right people and go to the right events. You probably aren't going to meet a lot of motivated sellers at the $ 400-a-night events, not that I go to those.

Check out **WWW.JIMPELLERIN.COM** for more articles on Lease Options and Real Estate Investing.

Chapter 7. Tenant Financing

In this section, we want to talk about the financials that you need to consider when dealing with a tenant buyer. I am talking about financials at the start of the transaction, financials through the term of the deal, and the financials required to close the deal. This is not to be confused with the ways you will make money with Lease Options.

In this section, we are going to look at the decisions you must make regarding all of financials related to a Lease Option. How you are going to treat all that money? How much money are you going to collect from the tenant? How are you going to apply those funds? How are you going to approve that tenant based on the financing they must get at the end of the deal?

The first financial component is the upfront deposit. There are a few things that you must consider when you are looking at the deposit. First, is it a deposit or an option credit or an option consideration, or a down payment? All these terms mean the same thing. However, you also need to be aware of how the banks would view these deals. There are a few issues that you might run into depending on how you treat that upfront deposit.

The next financial component happens throughout the length of the Lease Option arrangement. These financial items are the monthly credits and monthly profits. Profit is not a tenant consideration even though the tenant is paying you the profit.

During the term of the Lease Option program, there is an amount that you may have added to the monthly payment that may be credited towards their purchase, should the tenant decide to buy. When considering adding this credit to the tenant's lease payment, you have to make sure that it's something the tenants can afford. You want to make sure that the total amount isn't so high that the tenants are going to be moving out in 6 months because they can't keep paying that amount.

The base monthly payment is set, so that it covers all the housing costs. There's also the credit component that will be added to the monthly payment so that you will be crediting the tenant when they purchase the property. And, finally, the other monthly piece is the profit. The monthly profit is an additional amount that you add to provide a reasonable overall profit for the deal. You may want to add this monthly profit because the end price is so low due to low appreciation in that area.

The third financial component that you need to be concerned with is the down payment the tenant must save. When it comes time for the tenant to buy the property, they are buying it for an already agreed to price. They will be using the initial deposit and the monthly credits as the down payment.

The down payment that you might be helping the tenant save for is 5% of the purchase price. However, you might want to consider helping them save 10%. The additional savings would allow for some money for the closing costs, which can be anywhere from 2% to 4% of the purchase price.

You want to make sure that all the contracts are structured such that when the tenant goes to purchase the property, they have enough money available to complete the transaction. You will have to help the tenant out with all that planning and preparation and the accumulation of the down payment for the eventual purchase and closing.

7.1 Tenant Deposit

The first tenant buyer's financial item that you need to be concerned with is the deposit.

The deposit, or the option consideration as it is sometimes referred to, is the amount of money that the tenant is going to put down to be able to move into a particular property. This option consideration gives the tenant the right to purchase this property at some time in the future for an agreed-to price.

For example, if we have a property worth $300,000 and the future price is $330,000, a 5% down payment would require that the tenant saves $16,500. The initial deposit that they pay let's say it's $10,000 would go towards that down payment for the eventual purchase of that house.

There are a few things to take into consideration when determining the amount of the deposit/option fee.

The first thing is the income of the tenant. The second thing is your comfort level or risk associated with the tenant. The third thing is the price of the home.

If that tenant is only making $20,000 a year and is trying to purchase a property for $300,000, and can only put down $2,000, that's not going to work. The minimum deposit that I ask for in my area is $10,000. But sometimes there are exceptions. For example, I may allow a smaller deposit depending on the credit capability of the person and their income. I would then set up a payment program to collect the balance.

I have one gentleman right now, and his credit score is 720, which is an excellent credit score. He has two incomes — one as an employee and the other as a side business. However, the banks won't recognize his side business. But through the due diligence that we have done, we know that he makes twice as much as what the banks think he makes. So, what we did is we have a Lease Option arrangement where he is paying $2,000 a month for his Lease Option payment. He only put down a small deposit of $2,000, and we are collecting another $1,000 a month for his deposit. So, because of his income, we negotiated a lower initial deposit.

But you really want a minimum deposit of $10,000, unless you have exceptions like I just mentioned. But the deposit amount could also depend on the price of the house.

For example, another deal I have is for a property that we paid almost $500,000 for. This is an expensive *Lease option agreement* for my area. Now I only asked him to put down $10,000. Between him and his wife, they make about $200,000 a year. So, they have the income to support it, but at the same time I'm very concerned that he doesn't have enough equity in the deal, and he has missed a few payments.

We are now coming to where it's time to close the deal, and I don't think his credit is good enough to qualify. I am concerned that he may walk away from the agreement since he only has $10,000 in the deal. Now he does have about $26,000 in credits that he has accumulated over the last three years, but I am still concerned that we may have to sell and not get our money out of this deal.

For high-end homes, I should have probably asked for a $20,000 deposit or maybe even a $25,000 deposit. A rule of thumb that some investors use when determining the amount of deposit to ask for is a minimum of 5% down.

Some people think that if they had 5% to put down, they wouldn't need us. And sometimes that's the case. But to qualify for a mortgage, lenders will look at the income of the applicant, the down payment they have, and their credit score. So, it's not just how much down payment they have. Make sure you explain that to your prospective client.

One important point to make is that, <u>it's better to have an empty unit than a bad tenant.</u>

If you put somebody in a property and they have only given a deposit of $1,000, or even worse $500, and they are paying $500 a month to accumulate that down payment, there's not a lot of "skin in the game" so to speak. My experience has been that most of those people are a terrible risk.

When I was first starting my Lease Option business, I had a lot of tenant buyers default on me because I allowed them to enter into an arrangement without a high enough deposit. Again, that minimum may be lower for a specific area.

For example, in one city that I invest in, you can purchase a home for $100,000. In that city, I might allow a minimum of only $5,000 for the deposit. In other towns where my homes are worth $300,000, I require a minimum of $10,000.

7.2 Tenant Monthly Payments

The next tenant financial component that we will look at is the monthly payment.

The monthly payment is the monthly *lease payment* that the tenant must pay. When setting the lease payment amount, you want to make sure it covers several things.

Monthly Costs

The first thing is you want to ensure that the monthly payment covers all your monthly costs. The monthly amount includes the mortgage principal, mortgage interest, taxes, and insurance

(PITI). Those are all the typical costs associated with owning a home.

At a bare minimum, the monthly lease payment that the tenant is paying has to cover these costs. You never want to be out of pocket. You never want to have negative cash flow when doing these deals. I've heard some investors say that they can't find any good deals, so they are OK with negative cash flow. They say they will make it up in the back end when they sell. This is the wrong approach. There are all kinds of ways to make sure that you have a positive cash flow in these arrangements.

Monthly Credit

The second component that makes up the monthly payment is the monthly credit. The monthly credit is an amount that you add to the monthly payment that will eventually go toward the tenants' down payment when they buy. This is a form of forced savings for the tenant buyer.

Let's say, for example, the tenant buyer needs a down payment of $20,000 to purchase the home. They give an initial deposit of $10,000. This means they must save another $10,000. This would require an additional monthly credit payment of approximately $300 a month spread over 36 months if you are using a 3-year term.

What you would do in this case is add that $300 to their monthly payment. This accumulated credit will be applied to the down payment when they purchase. Never allow the tenant to save this amount on their own and not pay you the monthly credit payment.

Firstly, you want to make sure that that credit amount is paid to you since it also provides you with cash flow.

Secondly, the tenant hasn't been able to save for their down payment up until now, so don't leave it up to them to save for the balance. You have to make sure the money is there when it comes time to close in 3 years. Sure, they might have been able to save the initial $10,000 for the deposit, but now they are paying a higher monthly lease payment in addition to all their other expenses. So, it might be more difficult for them to save.

You want to make sure that you are collecting ALL the money that will be used for the down payment when it comes time to purchase. Don't leave anything to chance.

MONTHLY PROFIT

The third component of the monthly payment is profit. Some people think you can't add anything to the monthly payment, other than what is required to cover your costs. Sure, you can. You are trying to make a good return on these investments. But some investors are charging so much additional profit, that it's outrageous. I'm not suggesting that you do that.

Your overall profit is based on the eventual sale of the property. The sale price can be based on the estimated appreciation. But it may be that you are concerned about where the economy is going and what the property would be worth at the end of the lease option period. One of the things you can do is reduce the sale price and increase the monthly payments. This would allow you to continue to make the profit you want while keeping the backend sale price within reason. For example, you could add $200, $300, or $400 to the monthly payment and decrease the eventual sale price of the property by $7,000 to $14,000 or more.

If you decide that you are going to increase the monthly payment this way and decrease the final purchase price, you must make sure the tenant can afford to make this higher monthly payment. You need to evaluate a tenant using the traditional bank's evaluation process.

When evaluating a tenant's financial capability, I use the standard gross debt service (GDS) and total debt service (TDS) ratios. When using the GDS, I don't allow their full house payment to exceed 32% of their gross income. So, if their lease payment is $2,000 a month, they must make approximately $6,000 per month or $72,000 per year. That's the minimum income they need to be earning.

I also look at their TDS and won't approve anyone whose TDS is higher than 40%. So, if the applicants have car payments, credit card payments, etc. totaling $1,500 and their lease payment is $2,000, they, would have a monthly commitment of $3,500. This means the minimum income required is $8,750 per month or $105,000 per year ($105,000*40%/12)

7.3 Tenant Down Payment

The last financial component that you need to be concerned with is the tenant's down payment. What I am referring to here is not the initial deposit payment but rather the down payment the tenant needs to accumulate for their eventual purchase.

The key to the down payment is that you must make sure that the tenants have accumulated a large enough down payment so that they can purchase the property. This down payment is calculated based on the purchase price.

For example, let's say the purchase price is $300,000, and the tenant has to accumulate 5% for the down payment, which is $15,000. Assuming they gave you a $10,000 upfront deposit, then you have to collect another $5,000 over the length of the contract.

This down payment that the tenant is saving is the down payment that they are going to use to purchase the property. Sometimes they think that these accumulations of deposits and credits are refundable. They believe that if they don't buy the property, they get their money back. In my transactions, if they do not buy the property, then they do not get their money back.

The amount of money that the tenant contributed to their down payment, through the initial deposit and the monthly credits, is not refundable. Make sure that they know this. Make sure that there is a waiver or statement that you get them to sign up front, stating that it is non-refundable.

Your tenants may decide that they aren't going to purchase the property. By doing so, they walk away and waive their right to their initial deposit and their monthly credits.

For example, I had one couple that put down $20,000 and moved into the property. A few months later, they decided they didn't want the property. They left and didn't notify us. They tried to get their deposit back by getting their lawyer to come after us. But they lost since the contracts were clear that the deposit was non-refundable.

The down payment that the tenants are accumulating must be an amount that the bank would accept as enough down payment for the purchase.

For example, I mentioned 5% is a minimum amount that most banks require. But maybe the tenants are self-employed, and perhaps the bank that you are dealing with or the banks in your area require 10% or 20% from a self-employed individual.

You must consider this when determining how much of a down payment the tenant should be saving for. Especially in today's market, where it is harder for people to get qualified for a mortgage.

The other thing you may want to consider is that you may want the tenant to save additional money for the closing costs.

Closing costs could be as high as 2%. So it may be that you want the tenant to save 7%. 2% of that can be used for closing costs and 5% for the down payment.

Remember to make sure you are evaluating the tenant's credit along the way, using a good credit management program. You want to make sure that they are ready to purchase when we need them to buy the house.

You must keep good records of the deposit and of the credits that have been paid.

For example, when the tenants write you a check for the $10,000 deposit, make sure that they keep the statement or that they get their bank statement that shows they wrote a check for $10,000. Take a picture of that check and keep it on file. You also want to keep track of their monthly payments.

There must be a clear way to show the lender that the down payment was collected from the tenant.

Check out **WWW.JIMPELLERIN.COM** for more articles on Lease Options and Real Estate Investing.

Chapter 8. What Types of Contracts Do You Use?

In this section, we want to talk about the different contracts involved in a Lease Option transaction.

Remember, there are several parties involved in a Lease Option transaction. There is a seller, an investor, and a tenant buyer. And there is yourself, the person or the company that's brokering the deal.

There are a few different ways to do the transaction. You could do a property-first, a tenant-first, or a Sandwich Lease Option.

There will be several contracts required between the different parties.

Lease Agreement

A *lease agreement* is required. It will be set up differently, depending on if it's a sandwich lease or not. The *lease agreement* may be between the tenant and yourself or between the tenant and the owner of the property.

Agreement of purchase and sale

Another agreement that you may have in place is an *agreement of purchase and sale* (APS). The *agreement of purchase and sale* will be used at the start of a transaction if you or an investor is buying the property. That's for a standard real estate transaction.

An APS is also used for the sale of the property to the tenant buyer at the end of the lease option term. That *agreement of purchase and sale* would be drawn up between the tenant and possibly yourself or the owner, depending on how you structure these deals.

OPTION AGREEMENT

Another agreement you might put in place would be an option agreement. The option agreement means that the tenant buyer has the option to purchase the property from either you or the owner directly, depending on if it's a sandwich lease or not.

In a sandwich lease option, it would be set up such that there's an option agreement between the seller and myself and between myself and the tenant buyer. To complete the transaction, the tenant buyer would exercise their option, and I would assign that option agreement to the seller.

If it's NOT a sandwich lease option, the option agreement would be directly between the tenant buyer and the seller.

JOINT VENTURE AGREEMENT

Another agreement you will probably need is a *joint venture agreement*. I do a lot of joint ventures. My joint ventures are set up with the owner so that I do ALL of the management work, maintenance, and repairs. I also work with the tenant buyers to prepare them to get approved for their eventual purchase.

The *joint venture agreement* is between the owner and me. Their only contribution is they would own the property and hold the mortgage on the property.

Now let's cover these contracts in more detail in the following sections.

8.1 THE LEASE AGREEMENT

The first contract that we are going to look at is the *lease agreement*.

A *lease agreement* is an agreement between the tenant and another party that says that the tenant has the right to live in the unit as long as they follow specific rules. Those rules include such things as paying the rent, not damaging the property, and keeping the property in good repair.

I use local *lease agreement*s. These are *lease agreement*s that were created by the municipality or by the local real estate board. I don't try to do anything fancy with the *lease agreement* itself. I use an addendum to add any additional rules.

The *lease agreement* is between the tenant and either you, as a property manager, or between the tenant and the owner. This will depend on the strategy you are using and how you want to set up the contracts.

If I was doing a sandwich lease, then I would have two *lease agreements*. I would have one *lease agreement* between myself and the tenant where the tenant would be leasing the property directly from me. I would also have another *lease agreement* between the owner and me. The agreement I have with the tenant would be a *sub-lease agreement*.

If I'm not doing a sandwich lease, and if I'm doing a joint venture with the owner, I would have the tenant lease directly from the owner. I would have a *property management agreement* or a *joint venture agreement* with the owner that says I'm allowed to manage this property on the owner's behalf.

When writing up the *lease agreement*, you want to make sure that you have provisions specifically for the *Lease option agreement*. For example, all my Lease Options are maintenance-free, which means the tenant is responsible for all maintenance and all repairs.

As mentioned, I have an addendum to the *lease agreement*. In the addendum, it specifies that the tenant is responsible for all repairs. Originally, I had a limit on repair costs, and the tenant was only responsible for the first $1,000 or $2,000 of repairs. I have since revised the addendum to indicate that the tenant is responsible for all repairs.

I am still concerned about whether the tenant is making those necessary repairs and whether the repairs would be done correctly. For example, if there was significant water damage (a flood) and they can't afford to make the repairs, the damage would become even worse if left unattended.

Since we also have insurance on the property, we might make an insurance claim for any significant damage to make sure that the work is being done and it is being done correctly. We would do this even though the contract says that the tenants are 100% responsible for all repairs. So, in the case of significant repairs, such as flood, fire, furnace repairs, roof replacement, or whatever the situation, we try and get insurance to cover it.

However, an insurance claim may affect the insurance premium. So, I would have a clause in the contracts that says if there is a need to repair any significant damages through insurance, we will do that. However, if the insurance premiums for their property go up as a result of that claim, their monthly lease payment will also increase to cover those additional insurance costs.

The monthly lease amount indicated in the *lease agreement* is set to cover all the costs associated with owning the property, as well as any credit that we want to add to that payment and any additional profit that we might want to put in there as well.

For example, if it costs $1,500 to cover the mortgage, taxes, and insurance, and the tenant is putting in $300 a month as credit. That's a total of $1,800 a month payment. And let's say we have an additional $200 as profit. Now the monthly payment is $2,000 a month. That's the amount that we will use as their lease payment, and that's the amount that we put on the *lease agreement*. If the insurance premium increases by $25, the *Lease agreement* would be amended to change the lease payment to $2,025 a month.

Some people structure the arrangement so that they keep the credit payments separate from the lease payments. They say that it's easier to show the credits when it comes time to qualify the tenant for their purchase. There may also be some legal reasons for doing it that way in your area. I don't do it that way. I make it all in one payment.

The nice thing about including the credit into the lease payment as one is that, if for any reason the tenant decides they don't want to buy and they don't want to move out, they are still paying a relatively high monthly rent payment. If they don't move out and continue renting, all my monthly costs are still covered, and I have a pretty good cash flow, even as a rental.

The other thing to think about when you are drawing up a *lease agreement* is always to make sure the lease term is the same as the term of the other contracts.

For example, if it's a three-year *Lease option agreement*, I have the lease specify that it's for three years as well. And if the tenant decides to move out before the end of that lease period, they are still bound by the landlord-tenant act. You can recover as many costs as the landlord-tenant act allows you to on the three-year lease.

Even though this "transaction" is called a Lease Option or a Rent to Own, you are still bound by the landlord-tenant act since the tenant is renting.

Make sure you understand what the landlord-tenant act rules are so that you're not violating any laws when you implement your *lease agreement*.

The way I ensure that I am working within the rules of my local landlord-tenant act is quite simple. I use the standard *lease agreement* for that community, town, or city. This approach ensures that my lease is following the standard rules and guidelines. Make sure you have the right addendum attached, which specifies that the tenant is responsible for all the maintenance and repairs.

8.2 OPTION AGREEMENT AND APS

The next two contracts we are going to look at is the *Agreement of purchase and sale* and the Option to Purchase Agreement.

The reason we are covering both agreements together is that they are the agreements that are going to allow the tenant buyer to purchase the property.

OPTION TO PURCHASE AGREEMENT

So, let's start with the Option to Purchase Agreement. The Option to Purchase Agreement is an agreement that allows the tenant buyer to purchase the property at some time in the future at an agreed-to price.

For example, if the tenant has an option to purchase the property at $330,000, we will have an agreement that says that this tenant buyer can buy this property at $330,000 on or before a specified date. That date is usually three years later in my deals.

Now there may be reasons why you might not want a tenant to purchase a property before the three years, and they can only purchase the property at that date specified and not before.

For example, rather than saying "three years on or before," you state that only on that "specified date" can they exercise that option.

The advantages of specifying an exact date and not before are that if the tenant decides to exercise the option a year earlier, you will lose a lot of potential profits from principal paydown and any monthly profit. Sure, maybe you can use the money you get from the sale and go and do another deal, but it's just something to keep in mind when you're setting up your business model. You should decide if you are going to allow a tenant buyer to purchase that property before the term ends.

In a sandwich *lease agreement*, the option agreement would be between the tenant buyer and your company. There would also be another option agreement between your company and the owner of the property.

What happens in a sandwich lease is, if the tenant buyer exercises their option with you, you would, in turn, exercise your option agreement with the owner, since you also have an option agreement with them. Again, this is only for the sandwich Lease Option deals. This is a very complicated scenario and should only be done with the help of your lawyer.

So, in this case, I would probably assign my option agreement that I have with the owner to the tenant buyer. Or I could assign the option agreement that I have with the tenant buyer to the owner. Either way, I would make sure that the money I have left in the deal for my profits would be included in the assignment agreement as an assignment fee.

Keep in mind, the option agreement does not allow anybody to purchase a property. The option agreement only gives someone the **option** to purchase the property at that price.

Once someone exercises an option agreement, it should be replaced with the *Agreement of purchase and sale*. Banks don't understand what option agreements are. They need to see a transaction represented in an *Agreement of purchase and sale*.

AGREEMENT OF PURCHASE AND SALE

The *Agreement of purchase and sale* must specify the same amount that was specified in the option agreement as the *option price*. For example, if the option price in the option agreement was $330,000, this is the sale price that must be in the *Agreement of purchase and sale*.

The other thing you must specify in the *agreement of purchase and sale* is how the down payment was paid. It would show the deposit and the monthly credits from the monthly lease payments.

Some banks allow us to show the deposits in this way. However, the banks will want to see some records showing that the buyers have made those payments. What we do is produce a report showing their payment history. Some banks won't do Lease Option transactions at all.

In summary, the *agreement of purchase and sale* is what shows the transaction between the tenant buyer and the owner. The option agreement is only there to allow the tenant the option to purchase the property. The tenant will exercise that option through another document called the

Exercise of Options document. So really, there are three documents required when using an option agreement approach.

Keep in mind; if this is a sandwich lease, there would be two sets of contracts. Again, this can get very complicated between exercising options, assigning options, and drawing up the *agreement of purchase and sale*. Sometimes you may even have a double closing. The key is to keep all this simple.

Another way to close a Lease Option deal is NOT to use option agreements at all. The way I now do lease purchases is I use an *Agreement of purchase and sale* at the start of the transaction. It's no longer a situation where the tenant has an option to buy the property, and the owner has an obligation to sell it. It's now a firm commitment by both parties to complete this transaction in 3 years. The APS is conditional upon two things.

The transaction is conditional upon inspection and financing. The beautiful thing about the financing is since we worked with the tenant buyer over the three years helping them repair their credit, we are in a position to know if that tenant is in a good position to be able to purchase that property before we even go to the bank to apply for the mortgage.

In conclusion, those are the contracts that allow the tenant buyer to purchase the property. For the *Agreement of purchase and sale*, I usually use local Real Estate Board documents.

8.3 Property Management and Joint Venture Agreements

The next two contracts we will cover are the *Property management agreement* and the *Joint venture agreement*.

The reason why I group these two contracts is that these are the two types of contracts that are between my company and the owner.

Joint Venture Agreement

The *Joint venture agreement* lays out who is doing what in the Lease Option transaction. The *Joint venture agreement* describes what each party is responsible for.

For example, in my joint ventures, I'm responsible for a lot of things. I'm responsible for finding the tenant and for making sure the tenant has a deposit. I'm responsible for the ongoing management of the tenant. If there are any problems with that tenant, I take care of them. If there are any problems with the tenant not paying, I still pay the owner.

If this is a tenant-first lease purchase, I'm also responsible for finding the property. I'm responsible, with my Realtor, to make sure that the tenant goes out and finds the right property.

I'm responsible for making sure that we do our due diligence on the tenant at the start and that we do a credit check and a background check. We also make sure that the tenant has the necessary deposit. We collect rent every month. We do all the property management.

The owner is the other party in the joint venture and is responsible for owning the house, holding the mortgage, and making sure that the appropriate insurance is in place.

For example, if we are buying a $300,000 home, and if the lender requires a 20% down payment, then the investor must have necessary down payment plus 2% for closing costs. So roughly $66,000 is needed to purchase a $300,000 home.

From an investor's perspective, though, there's not much that they must do beyond buying the property. They have to get approved for financing. They have to purchase the property, which means they'll have to go and execute an *Agreement of purchase and sale*. Then they'll have to go to the lawyer's and close the transaction.

Again, there are not a lot of activities for the investor to do. They may have to spend 2 or 3 hours driving to their mortgage company and their lawyers and the real estate company. And I even coordinate all that for them.

What I try to do is make the whole process as hands-off a transaction as possible for the investor. I am trying to create a passive investment strategy for my investors, almost like a guaranteed investment certificate.

The *Joint venture agreement* also specifies that the investor and I will split the profits 50/50. That's my standard arrangement. Sometimes I might go lower on my share if the investor has reasons why they would want me to go lower. But typically, we will split the total profits.

Property Management Agreement

The other contract that I may use with an investor, instead of a joint venture, is a *Property management agreement*.

In the *property management agreement*, I describe what I would do as a property manager. These are the same things specified in the *Joint venture agreement*. I will manage the tenant, collect the rent, handle all repairs, and pay the rent regardless if the tenant pays me or not. I will withhold a certain amount of money when the tenant pays me because that's how I get paid as a property manager. I will only pay the owner the balance after I get paid my property management fees.

For example, let's say that there are $1,500 in costs, but the tenant is also paying an additional $500 to cover profit and their lease option credits. This means their total monthly payment is $2,000.

I will collect the $2,000 from the tenant but only remit to the owner, or their bank, the $1,500, which is enough to cover the monthly costs. I keep the balance of $500, which is pre-paying me my portion of the 50/50 split.

The *property management agreement* specifies that I will get 50% of the profits for managing the property. The terms are the same as the *Joint venture agreement*.

There may be reasons why you would use a *property management agreement* instead of a *Joint venture agreement*. One of those reasons may be a tax consideration.

It may be that you are required to pay tax on services that you provide. So, if you're using a *property management agreement*, it may be deemed that you are providing property management services, and those services are subject to tax. This tax will vary depending on your location.

In a *joint venture agreement*, I'm partnering with the owner, and therefore there is probably no service tax required. You are best to talk to a tax expert before deciding on which contract might work better in your area.

You will need to decide as to which agreement works best for you in your location. The essence of both contracts is the same. Both agreements define the relationship between you or your company, and the owner of the property.

Check out **WWW.JIMPELLERIN.COM** for more articles on Lease Options and Real Estate Investing.

Chapter 9. Managing a Lease Option

In this next section, we will cover the activities that need to be done to manage the Lease Option arrangement.

Property Management

First, you will be responsible for the ongoing management of the property and the management of the tenant.

Ongoing management means making sure that the tenant is paying on time. Making sure that if there are any maintenance or repairs required, they were done and done correctly. Making sure that there are no problems with the property itself and that if there are any *significant* repairs that need to be done that they are being done and not ignored.

I have had tenants who have put a new deck on the back of the property. I have tenants who have added a new bathroom. Both these renovations could increase the value of the property. But we had to make sure that all that work was done according to code. And we had to make sure that the tenants checked with us first, before doing the work.

You also have to make sure that, if there are any outstanding rent payments, that you are following the proper collection and eviction processes. Also, if the tenants have missed a payment, make sure that you still pay the owner as a part of a *joint venture agreement*.

MANAGEMENT OF MAINTENANCE AND REPAIRS

In my contracts, the tenant buyers are responsible for ALL the maintenance and repairs. However, there are times when extensive repairs may be required.

What if the roof starts leaking, and we find out that it needs replacing? A new roof requires a huge cash outlay. Or maybe it's some other major repair, and the tenant can't afford it. We don't want the property to suffer as a result of that required repair not being done.

What we do in this situation is, if the insurance doesn't cover it, we would pay for the repair on behalf of the tenant but add the costs to the future purchase price.

For example, if the expected purchase price is $300,000 and a significant repair cost me $5,000, I would add that $5,000 to the purchase price, making it now $305,000. This way, the property gets repaired, and I get to recover the cost of the repair.

CREDIT MANAGEMENT

The other part of managing a Lease Option arrangement is credit management.

You must make sure that the tenant is continually trying to repair and improve their credit. You must make sure they know what to do. You will take a snapshot of their existing credit situation, and then you will work with them and monitor their progress over the life of the arrangement.

So, these are the three types of management that I'm going to cover in this chapter.

9.1 PROPERTY MANAGEMENT

The most important part of managing a Lease Option deal is property management.

Property management is all about managing the property. There you go. Easy explanation.

What that means is making sure that you manage the *property* and the *tenant* properly. That means everything from taking care of the necessary repairs, making sure the tenant is making their payments, and just making sure that everything is being managed in an orderly and professional fashion.

As mentioned earlier, there is a *lease agreement* between the tenant and my company or between the tenant and the owner. The *lease agreement* states that the tenant must remit rent payments to us every month. And yes, believe it or not, the tenants don't always pay on time. If this happens, we have penalties in place for any late or missed payments.

It's crucial to remember that tenants will tell you all kinds of stories about why they can't pay on time. You need to put stringent rules in place that fits within the laws of your landlord-tenant act.

What we do is we have a policy in place that, if a tenant doesn't pay on the first of the month, or if their payment is late for any reason, or if their payment returns due to non-sufficient funds, we send out an eviction notice the very next day.

For example, if the rent is due on the 1st of the month and we get a payment that bounced on the 5th of the month, we issue an eviction notice on the 6th of the month.

I have heard all kinds of stories from tenants — everything from deaths to divorces to medical problems to companies moving to companies changing payments, etc.

Sure, some of these stories might be true. But I tell my tenants that they can call my bank and talk to the bank about why I can't pay the mortgage because they haven't paid me. I also explain to my tenants that they are borrowing money from me when they don't make a payment.

When a tenant doesn't make payment for whatever reason, I tell them to go out and borrow the money. And when they tell me that they can't borrow the money, I explain to them that they just borrowed it from me, since I still had to pay the owner or the bank. Remember, my commitment to the owner is that I will pay them no matter if the tenant pays me or not.

So, in essence, the tenant is borrowing the money from me by not paying their rent, and I have to use my funds to pay the bank or the owners.

Don't get swayed by any stall tactics by the tenant. If this keeps going on, you may have to take legal action, and you may have to terminate the Lease Option arrangement.

I've done this a few times, where I have had to evict the tenant for non-payment. And yes, they lose all their deposits and all their credits. So, the tenants are very motivated to stay in the transaction.

I know I'm a pushover sometimes too. And I don't want to go out and start looking for another candidate to replace this tenant. It's too much of a hassle. So, I have made some concessions where I have allowed some of the rent payments to go unpaid for one month or two months. Sometimes the landlord-tenant act requires this much time to evict anyway. There is a process you must follow to evict the tenants.

I have one city where I can get somebody out in 30 days and another city where it usually takes me 60 to 90 days. It depends on the rules in each location.

The other thing you want to make sure of is that you have a penalty in place for late payments. Again, it depends on what your landlord-tenant act will allow, but I charge $100 for any NSF payment, and I charge $100 for any late fee.

If the tenant is paying me $2,000 a month and they don't pay on time, or even if they call and ask me to delay depositing their payment, I charge them $100, so the amount due is now $2,100.

If they bounce a check, I also charge them for any of the fees my bank charges me. For example, if the bank charges me $25 for a bounced check, the fees that the tenant must pay is now $100 plus the bank charge of $25, which is $125. Make sure you're diligent in collecting those fees. And make sure you don't violate any landlord-tenant rules with these fees.

The other part of this non-payment to be concerned about is the *Option Agreement*. I specify in the *Option Agreement* that for the tenant to get the credit amount, they must pay their lease payment on time and that it clears. So, if they bounce a check or if they don't pay on time, they don't get their credit. They would have to make up those credits to be able to close the transaction because they need all the credits to be able to purchase.

From a property management perspective, you have to make sure that the tenants are paying on time and that the owners are paid on time. It's all about the collection of money.

9.2. MAINTENANCE

The next part of managing the property is the maintenance of the property itself.

In my agreements, the tenant buyer is responsible for ALL maintenance associated with the property. What that means is, if there is any damage or if there are any repairs that are needed, the tenant is responsible.

For example, if there's a door that needs replacing or a window that needs replacing, or if there is some plumbing work required, the tenant is responsible for repairing it. Also, if the property has appliances, and these appliances break down, the tenant is responsible.

You also have to make sure that, even though the tenant is responsible for these repairs, the repairs get done. It may be that the tenant can't make those necessary repairs because they can't afford to. You may need to make the repairs on their behalf.

You can always work out some deal with the tenant where you pay for the repairs and add it to their monthly payment or add it to their purchase price. Something needs to be arranged so that you recover those costs. You don't want the property to go into a state of disrepair, which could make the problem even worse. And you don't want to have to pay for those repairs.

For example, let's say a window broke and was not repaired. And now the hardwood floor in the unit is rotting away because of rain damage. Now the floors need to be replaced.

I had one unit that was in such disrepair that, by the time I got in there to repair it, it cost me $30,000 to fix everything. In that situation, I was an absentee landlord, but that's another topic for another discussion.

You want to make sure that the property is being adequately maintained.

For major repairs, maybe they can be handled under your insurance.

For example, if a water main breaks and suddenly, there's a flood in the basement. Or let's say your furnace stops or blows up. Or what if your roof was damaged because of some natural disaster?

If any major repair can be handled by using your insurance, you should look at going that route to repair.

If there is an increase in the insurance because of your claim, then you will have to work out an arrangement with the tenant buyer that they will cover the increased insurance premium.

As discussed, we are only collecting enough from the tenant buyer to cover the costs that were initially identified. For example, if the insurance policy is $1,200 a year, and after the claim, the premium increases to $1,800, then the tenant would have to kick in another $50 a month to cover that $600 increase.

You have to make sure that the property is being maintained properly. You could do this by scheduling a visit every six months or a year.

You'd be surprised at what your visits may uncover. I have had visits where the property is in immaculate condition. I have also had visits where the property is not being maintained very well. We had to remind the tenant that the contract states that they are responsible for all maintenance and repairs.

In conclusion, maintenance and repairs are a crucial part of managing a property. Repairs are to be taken care of when they happen, and you, as a landlord, must monitor it to make sure such repairs are being done when needed.

9.3 Credit Management

The last thing we will look at concerning managing a Lease Option arrangement is credit management.

Credit management is about getting a tenant buyer in the right credit position so that they can purchase the property at the end of their two or three-year agreement.

The first thing you need to do is to take a snapshot of the tenant's current credit situation, so you know their starting point. Once you know their starting point, then you can determine what needs to be done to ensure that the tenant will get approved in three years.

So first, you will need to look at their credit report. You will need to know the prospect's starting score. You will look at all the trade lines on their report. You will look at all the outstanding debt that they have. You look at their credit ratios, both from a housing perspective and from a total debt perspective. And then you will put together a plan for them to follow.

Sometimes you will find that people will have too few or too many credit lines showing on their report. I have had clients in situations where they didn't have enough trade lines. What they needed to do in that case was go out and get a credit card, even if it was a secured credit card. Then they had to start making purchases with that card and start making regular payments.

The other extreme might be that they have too credit cards with high balances. So, you tell them to start paying down those credit cards. You work with them to come up with a plan to do this.

Sometimes you can send them for credit counseling if that makes sense. Credit counselors will help them restructure their debt and maybe even help them negotiate a paydown on those credit cards.

I had one tenant who went out and bought a brand-new truck that was costing him $1,000 a month. He lives out of town, but he works downtown, so his gas was another $500 a week. And then there was his insurance cost. I told him outright that he was not going to get approved if he doesn't sell his truck and buy a cheaper car for about half the price.

Sometimes tenants have to make tough short-term decisions if they want to be able to purchase the property in 3 years. If they don't make the necessary changes to their spending and if they don't improve their credit, they wouldn't be able to buy the property. If that happens, I will have to sell the house, and the tenant buyer will lose all the credits that they have earned, as well as their initial deposit.

You must be very strict and direct with tenant buyers. I get all my tenant buyers to sign up for our *Credit Management Program*. What I do is review their credit report at the start, when they first sign up. I go over it with the tenants and explain what needs to be done.

I review their credit report again every year and then again six months before closing. At that time, you should know whether they are in an excellent position to purchase the property or not.

When we review the tenant's credit, we are looking to see if they are paying down their debt, especially if they had a lot of credit card debt or a lot of revolving debt.

We also look to see where they are with their car payments and how many other payments they have. We also look at phone bills and student loans — basically, we look at everything on their credit report.

The other thing banks look at is income taxes. If people haven't filed their taxes, banks won't approve a loan. They want to confirm their income and at the same time and make sure they don't owe anything on their taxes.

These are things to look at when trying to position the tenant buyer to be able to purchase within their allotted time, which is usually three years. You have to make sure that the tenant buyers are doing everything to improve their credit score and reduce their debt and make sure their GDS and TDS ratios are okay to get them approved.

That concludes the chapter on managing a Lease Option arrangement.

Chapter 10. Getting the Tenant Approved

In this chapter, we are going to look at what's required to get a tenant buyer approved.

The tenant buyer is the person that is going to be renting the property and who is going to purchase a property in three years. That tenant buyer must be ready to buy the property at the end of the lease option agreement.

Down Payment

To purchase the property, the tenant must have a down payment that's going to be acceptable to the bank that will be approving them for the mortgage. The down payment includes the initial deposit plus the monthly credits.

Credit Score

The tenant buyer also needs a good credit score. You will have to work with the tenant buyers to make sure that their credit improves so that their credit *score* increases and is in line with what the banks want to see.

Mortgage Application

The mortgage application must be appropriately prepared. The mortgage application for a lease-purchase transaction is unique, and not a lot of lenders will allow it.

Getting the tenant buyer approved requires the proper down payment and accurately representing that down payment to the lender. You have to make sure the tenant buyer's credit score is at an acceptable level by showing them how to improve their credit through various methods and by preparing the actual mortgage application correctly so it's acceptable to the lender.

10.1 THE DOWN PAYMENT

The first thing you need to have when trying to get a buyer approved at the end of their lease-purchase term is the *down payment*.

If you recall, the tenant is going to make an application at the start of your process. As part of that application, they are required to pay an option fee or a deposit. They are going to provide you with an amount of money that will allow them to enter into the *lease option agreement*.

That amount of money will vary based on the cost of the house, the payment capability of the applicant, and on the current credit situation of the applicant. I'm always looking for a minimum of $5,000 on my lower-end units.

I usually ask for a minimum of $10,000 in some of my higher-end units in larger cities and have collected as much as $20,000.

That initial deposit will go towards the down payment for the purchase of the property at the time of closing. The down payment will be made up of that initial deposit plus a portion of the monthly lease payment that we set aside each month.

For example, if we are collecting $1,500 a month to cover the monthly costs, and if we need to collect an additional $300 credit to make up the down payment, their total monthly lease payment would be $1,800. The accumulation of these credits, over the term of the lease, will be applied to the down payment. So, the tenant is now paying $1,800 a month and earning a $300 a month credit towards their down payment. So, $300 x 36 is $10,800. And if we had collected an initial deposit of $10,000, they would have $20,800 to be used as their down payment.

The amount of money required for the down payment will depend on the purchase price, the credit score, the tenant's employment situation, and some other factors. If you position your tenant correctly, they will have the minimum down payment.

Sometimes the tenant may want to save more than the minimum amount required. Maybe they want to pay $400 a month or $500 a month. A larger payment means they would be saving for a bigger down payment for when it comes time to purchase, which means they would require a smaller mortgage, thus reducing their monthly payments after they purchase.

The minimum down payment most banks require is at least 5%. If the purchase price to the tenant buyer is $300,000, the banks will require a down payment of at least $15,000. In our example, if we collected $20,800, so they would have enough money for their down payment.

Sometimes that additional money could be used for closing costs. Closing costs include such things as legal costs, land transfer tax, title search, and title insurance. The tenant buyer must put aside enough money to make sure they can cover these expenses at the closing. The amount required for these costs varies from region to region. I try to put aside at least 2% of the purchase price to cover these closing costs.

Using our same example, if the purchase price is $300,000, they will need another $6,000. If we collected $20,800, and they needed $15,000 for the down payment and another $6,000 for closing costs, they are only short about $1,000.

So, there you have it. You should collect a minimum of 5% for the down payment and 2% for the closing costs, depending on the area.

10.2 Credit Score

The next thing you must do to prepare the tenants for their eventual purchase is to make sure they have a good credit score. Several things are required when preparing them for a good credit score.

You have to look at the number of credit lines they have on their credit bureau. What are the balances of each credit line? What is their payment activity against those credit lines? Are they making regular payments? What is the age of each credit line?

Obviously, the tenant was not able to get approved for a mortgage, otherwise, they wouldn't be in our program. They may have a good credit score, but they didn't have the necessary down payment. If they didn't have the down payment, but they did have a good credit score, then we wouldn't have much to do here. But, at the same time, you want to make sure that they maintain that good credit score.

NUMBER OF CREDIT LINES

I have had cases where people have applied for mortgages and cannot get approved for a mortgage because they did not have enough credit lines. For example, they have one credit card, which may make their credit look good. The banks would look at that and say that the credit score is over-inflated because they don't have enough credit lines, and therefore the credit score is not adequately represented. So, you have to make sure that, if they only had one credit line at the start, they go out and they get another loan or another credit card. I know it sounds strange, but it's true. Having too few credit lines is NOT good.

One of the things the tenant buyer could do is get a secured credit card where they put money down as security. But they have to make sure that they are making regular payments and that they keep that credit card in good standing.

So, the first thing is to make sure the tenant has enough credit lines

CREDIT BALANCES

The second thing is to keep the balances on those credit lines low. One of the things that greatly affect the credit score is having a high ratio on those credit lines. For example, let's say you have a credit card that has a limit of $3,000, and every time the balance is reported to the credit bureau, the balance is $2,900, or maybe it's even at the maximum. Or worse. I have seen people with $3,000 credit cards with a balance of $3,100, $3,200, or even $3,300. Credit card companies will allow people to go over their limits a bit. Credit card companies earn more interest that way. But it will affect their credit score.

Ideally, if they can get their credit balances down to 50%, that will improve their credit score. For example, if they have a credit card with a $3,000 limit, they should keep their balances at $1,500 or less.

Regular Payments

The third thing that the tenant can do to improve their credit score is to make sure that they are making consistent payments.

If they start missing payments, this will show up on their credit report. For example, if they are 30 days late in one credit line or maybe 60 days late in another credit line, this will be reported on their credit score.

It's better to make your credit card payment and then get a cash advance the next day. There will be a difference between the payment and the advance, but at least it shows that the payment was made on time and keeps their credit card in good standing.

So always, always, always make the payment on your credit card and then get a cash advance from your card if you need to. You can usually make the payment online and get the advance almost the same day. Just transfer money from your bank account to your credit card. Make a payment and then the next day or so, make a cash advance on that credit card and pull the money back into your bank account. At least you're maintaining regular credit card payments. You can even automate this process in some cases.

Tell the tenants never to let their credit card fall into three-month arrears. If they have 90-day arrears or even 60-day arrears, this will look bad. Usually, they can get away with one or two 30-day arrears, but there's no reason to have this if they have the cash available to make the payment and pull it out again the next day.

For example, if they have to make a $100 a month payment, make the $100 payment, and then the next day, they can take it back. Now they may only be able to get an advance for $90. But hopefully, they can find $10 a month to make the payment this way.

Again, it's crucial to keep their credit payments current and not miss any payments.

AGE OF CREDIT LINES

The age of the credit lines is also important. The sooner the tenant buyer can establish new credit lines, the sooner they can start managing it through the three-year cycle.

In summary, make sure that they have enough credit lines. Maybe 3 or 4, which consist of lines of credit, personal loans, car payments, and credit cards. They will need enough credit lines so that the banks can validate that they have good credit. You want to make sure that they keep their balances low, and you want to make sure that they are making regular, consistent payments.

10.3 THE APPLICATION

The last thing I want to cover that will help prepare the tenant to purchase is the actual application itself.

Remember, the first thing we talked about is the down payment. We need to make sure the down payment has been collected and properly represented on the *Agreement of Purchase and Sale (APS)*. When applying for a mortgage, an APS is required. All banks and lenders will want to see an

APS, and they will want to know the source of the down payment.

Now some lenders want to see that the down payment is seasoned. What this means is that the lender wants to see the money in the borrower's bank account for 60 days or more. Sometimes the down payment can be represented through a gift. If the tenant has a relative, they could get them to write a letter stating that they have given them the down payment as a gift.

Some banks understand how Lease Option works, and they will accept the payments as provided. What we do is produce a report for the banks. The report will state that we, as the property manager, have collected the initial $10,000 deposit from the tenant buyer on a specified date. Also, we have been receiving $300 a month from the tenant for every month after that.

Most banks that I have been dealing with will accept our letters, together with an account statement. The account statement details the payments and the credits that the tenant has made.

The APS states that the down payment is made up of an initial deposit of $10,000 and subsequent payments of $300 per month until closing, which is usually three years.

Most banks are not familiar with this type of down payment and, therefore, won't allow it. What I have done is I have found a bank that will do the Lease Options and use that lender for all my Lease Option transactions. As a result, we can get these Lease Option transactions approved relatively quickly.

Lenders are looking for that down payment. I am a mortgage broker, and I work with the banks directly to make sure that the tenants are pre-approved for the final purchase.

We are also working with tenant buyers through the term of the contract as part of the *Credit Management Program*. We do a credit check after the first six months, another one every year after, and a final check six months before the closing date.

When it comes to completing the application, we know that they have a down payment. We know that credit is in good standing. We see from the tenant's credit report what their credit score is. We also look at the credit ratios, which we mentioned earlier. These are the *total debt service* (TDS) and the *gross debt service* (GDS).

As described, the GDS is how much housing debt the tenant buyer would be carrying relative to their salary. And the TDS is how much total debt the tenant would be carrying relative to their salary. The total debt would include their housing debt as well as other debt associated with any of the credit cards or other loan payments they may have.

So, as long as those debt service ratios are in line with the lender allowed amounts and as long as the down payment is in line with the lender allowed amount, then we fill out the mortgage application.

This process usually goes quite smoothly because we have been working with the tenant all along. We have made sure the APS was completed properly. We have prepared the tenant properly, and everything should be fine. The application goes in, and it's approved without a problem.

As mentioned, some banks are looking for seasoned money. In this case, instead of showing the down payment as credits, we would deposit the funds into a trust account with the lawyer, 90 days before closing. This way, the bank will see that the deposit has been with the lawyer 90 days before closing.

In conclusion, several things need to be done to prepare the application properly. If you are not sure how to do this, make sure you work with someone who has experience closing Lease Option transactions. There are only a few people out there that have experience doing these types of transactions.

Check out **WWW.JIMPELLERIN.COM** for more articles on Lease Options and Real Estate Investing.

Chapter 11. Exit Strategies

In this section, I will cover the various exit strategies in Lease Option investing.

An exit strategy is what we plan on doing with the property at the end of the contract. What are the options?

The Tenant Buys

The primary exit strategy is that the tenant is going to buy. But that doesn't necessarily happen all the time, so we're faced with having to come up with other options. If the tenant doesn't buy, what do we do? There are several other things we can do.

Extend the Contract

We could extend the contract if, at the end of the current agreement, the tenant is not able to buy for whatever reason. Maybe their credit has not improved enough. Perhaps he doesn't have any money for closing costs. Whatever the reason. We will look at the situation and, depending on what we find, decide to extend the contract. So, what does that mean? For example, is there a new option price?

FIND A NEW TENANT

Another thing we could do is we could find another tenant buyer. I've had situations where, at the end of the term of the agreement, the tenant decided not to buy and left. What you could do in this situation is go out, find another tenant buyer and do another Lease Option with this new tenant buyer for another term.

SELL THE PROPERTY

A fourth option that I have used is that we sell the property outright on the open market. The owner of the property and I have made a lot of money from the deal, so we sell the property outright and make more profit from the sale.

So those are the four different exit strategies. We will explore these in more detail in the following sections.

11.1 TENANT BUYS

The first exit strategy for a Lease Option that we are going to look at is the one where the tenant buyer buys the property at the end of the term. Or possibly even before the term ends. <u>Buying the property is the preferred option.</u>

Let's assume we are doing a three-year Lease Option. Everything is moving along according to plan. The end of the three years has arrived. We have all the credits collected. The tenant buyer has been making their payments regularly. Their credit score has improved. They have the down payment. They have the financial capability to purchase. We have submitted the application, and the bank says everything is okay, so the tenant buys. That's the ideal situation.

As mentioned earlier, there's a lot that must be done to prepare for this situation to occur properly. But all the things that need to happen have happened. One thing we mentioned is that we have to make sure that the property is being adequately maintained and is in good condition. Proper property maintenance is so that when the appraiser comes in, the property gets the highest valuation.

The purchase is conditional upon financing. Always include that condition in the agreement. Although the tenant commits to purchasing the property in the APS, we still include this condition so that the tenants are in a position where they won't get sued if they can't get financing and, therefore, can't complete the purchase.

As part of the mortgage application, there is usually an appraisal that is required. An appraisal is required by the lender for most transactions these days. The tenant buyer needs to keep the property in good condition to ensure the property will appraise at the highest value.

Some of my tenants have made improvements, which increased the overall value of the house, which made it much easier for them to get approved because the house is now worth more than originally expected.

An inspection may also be required. The tenant has lived in the property for three years, so it's usually up to them whether they want to have an inspection done. We don't often have the inspection included as a condition. However, it's a good thing to get an inspection done because this will give the tenant information about the work required on the property. The inspection should be done at the start of the Lease Option agreement.

The tenant buyer should want to make sure that they are fine with the condition of the property before entering into the agreement.

So here it is three years later. We are going to get the tenant approved. They have their down payment saved. Their credit score is where it needs to be. The application has been properly prepared. The appraisal has been done, and the appraised amount is high enough for the purchase.

An inspection was done. Everything goes smoothly, and the tenant buys.

The title is then transferred from the owner's name into the tenant's name, who now becomes the owner. This part of the transaction happens just like any real estate transaction where a seller sells to a buyer.

So, the number one way to exit a Lease Option agreement is by the tenant purchasing the property. Now for me, this usually happens about 80% of the time where the tenant does buy the property.

So, what happens if they don't buy?

11.2 EXTEND THE CONTRACT

The next exit strategy we will cover is extending the contract. Here is the situation.

We have been working with the tenant now for three years. At the end of the three years, or actually, at six months before the end of the term, we do another evaluation of their credit score. What if their credit score isn't good enough yet? Meaning they haven't improved their credit to the point where we could get them a mortgage through the bank or any other lender.

We may have gone as far as trying to get a pre-approval with the lender to see if they might approve the tenant. We work with mortgage brokers. I'm a mortgage broker, so we can tell, based on our experience, whether that person will get approved or not.

If we can't get them approved, and we feel there's a high likelihood that they're not going to get approved, we start looking at options.

The first thing is to discuss it with the owner of the property.

Now, in some cases, the owner is me. In some cases, it's an investor, and in other cases, it's just the seller that we might be subletting through. We must go back to one of them, and we must have a discussion with them about the situation. We might suggest that they consider extending the contract.

Extending the contract is going to cost the tenant. There's no way around it. Because we have an owner, who is trying to make money from this property. Sometimes the owner is OK with extending the contract without additional cost to the tenant.

When I say it's going to cost the tenant more, what I mean is, if the tenant was going to buy the property at a specific price of, let's say $300,000, and now we have to extend the term for another year, we may have to add on an additional 2% or 3% on that price. So the new price might be $306,000 to $309,000. The extension costs the tenant buyer another $6,000 to $9,000.

Remember, most owners are now treating this as an investment and want to make money on their investment. And the only way we can do that when we extend the term is by increasing the purchase price that the tenant will have to buy the property at.

Some investors may say that they are making enough money on the mortgage principal paydown, and maybe there's already some profit built into the monthly payment, so we don't have to increase the price.

The owner may have been a very motivated seller who couldn't sell the property, and they don't need to make more money off a price increase, just as long as the tenant buys at the end of the new term.

Once I have a verbal agreement with the owner to extend the contract, we execute the new contracts. We usually amend the existing contract to change the closing date and the purchase price, if required.

What I will do is negotiate with the owner for a one-year extension but allow the tenant to purchase any time within that one year, assuming they can get approved before the 1-year term. It might be that their situation has improved after six months, then we would execute the transaction before the end of the 1-year term.

After getting an agreement from the owner to extend, I would then go to the tenant and explain the situation to them. All 3 parties must agree to this extension — the owner, the tenant buyer, and myself on behalf of my company. I also have to want to extend this contract since I will be the property manager.

That covers the exit strategy of *extending the contract*. Again, it's only an exit strategy we would look at if the number one exit strategy of the tenant purchasing is not a viable solution, and the tenant can't purchase.

11.3 Find a New Tenant

The next exit strategy we want to cover is getting a new tenant buyer. Here's the situation.

We have completed the Lease Option term, and the tenant is not able to buy. Now that situation doesn't have to wait for three years.

What happens sometimes is the tenant buyer decides to leave halfway through the term or maybe a year or two into the term. The tenant buyer could break their contract and leave at any time during the period. But, ultimately, the situation is the same. The tenant buyer is not going to buy the property or is not willing to buy the property or is not able to buy the property.

In any case, they've left the property, or maybe we even evicted them. I have had it happen where the tenant has gone through the entire term of the agreement and at the end of the period, decided not to purchase the property.

When the tenant leaves without purchasing the property, they lose their deposit and all the credits that they have earned. The way the contracts are written up is that the deposits and credits are only applied to the down payment **if they decide to buy**. If the tenant doesn't buy, they lose all these credits, but they leave anyway. I don't know why people do this, but it happens.

Next, what we do is we go out, and we market the property. Before doing that, I go back to the owner, explain the situation and ask them what they want to do. I tell the owner that there are benefits in finding another Lease Option tenant.

The benefit of this approach, from an owner's perspective, is that the upfront costs are now sunk costs since they were calculated into the original deal. These are all the upfront costs, such as the legal costs, land transfer costs, and title search costs. It is any costs incurred by the owner as a part of the original purchase.

So, if we do another 3-year deal with a new tenant, the return on the investment would be much higher because the property is already owned.

If the owner agrees to extend, we start marketing the property through our various marketing channels.

One of the things we can now do when we are marketing the property looking for a new tenant buyer is, we can offer them some incentives since we already have some built-in profits from the previous tenant.

For example, let's say the tenant was in the property for three years and had accumulated 5% for their down payment. And let's say that the amount was $20,000. Since the previous tenant didn't buy, we keep their deposit and credits, so the owner and I have $20,000 of additional profit that we can play around with.

We could keep that profit and start new. We could begin marketing the property on a new Lease Option with no incentives. Indeed, in a hot market, we could find lots of tenant buyers easily.

The other thing I've done is offered the prospective tenant buyers an incentive.

In addition to their $10,000 deposit, I would provide another $5,000 as an incentive credit or maybe even a $10,000 incentive credit. Whatever we feel makes sense to attract a new tenant buyer as quickly as possible. It's a way of using that $20,000 that the previous tenant left behind. We either use that profit for marketing, as an incentive, or keep it as profits.

So that's another exit strategy. Again, if the tenant buyer decides not to buy at the end of the term or at any time during the term and vacates the property. We then take that same property and go out and do another Lease Option and bring in another tenant buyer and make even more money.

And remember, this is not a strategy we want to do. Our preferred exit strategy is that the tenant buyer buys the property. It substantiates the product and the service that we are offering to our customers.

11.4 SELL THE PROPERTY

The last exit strategy we will discuss is selling the property.

Again, what we really want to happen here is that the tenant buyer buys the property. But, as mentioned, this doesn't always happen. Sometimes the tenant buyer isn't interested in buying the property, for whatever reason.

Sometimes people are forced to move again, or maybe they have decided they didn't like the house after all or perhaps they didn't like the area. I have had a few different reasons why the tenant buyer ended up not buying the property.

I had one couple that ended up getting divorced, and neither one of them could afford the payments by themselves. I've had another situation where the person didn't like the property anymore. And yet another case where the tenants did not like the area after living there for three years.

There are many reasons why the tenant buyer may decide not to purchase the property. And there are several alternative exit strategies, as previously described. This one focuses on selling the property at the end of the term or whenever the situation happens.

If this happens, I go back to the owner and explain the situation. I tell him that, since we are keeping the tenant buyer's credits, we made another 5% to 10% of additional profit on this property. One of the options is to sell and get out. Because we now have these unexpected profits, we could hire a Realtor and put it up for sale.

For example, let's say the tenant buyer was going to purchase the property for $300,000 and had earned $15,000 worth of credits that would have gone toward their down payment for the purchase of the property. Since the tenant has walked away from that, we now have $15,000 that we can use to hire a Realtor to go out and sell the property.

We then tell the Realtor we want to sell it so that we get the $300,000 we were expecting from the tenant buyer. If we have done our job right and priced the property right and if the market is where we thought it would be, then we should be able to get at least the $300,000 that the tenant was going to give us for the property. And that's after paying the Realtor.

I've had situations where we sold a property and got more than what the tenant buyer was going to pay.

To continue our example, it may be that the property is now worth $325,000 as fair market value. The Realtor puts it up for sale at $330,000, and we sell it for $320,000 as a result of the sale. Then the Realtor charges their 5% fee of $16.000, so we get $304,000. We thus made an extra $4,000 as a result of the sale, plus we keep the $15,000 credits that we received from the tenant.

One factor in deciding whether you sell or choose one of the other exit strategies is where the price is relative to the market. If the market would allow you to get very close to what your sale price was, then selling it may not be your best option because you would get less than what you would have received from the tenant buyer.

The way I present this to my investors is that if they really want to sell in a down market, and even though we may lose money on the sale, any loss will come out of my portion of the profits first. Obviously, this is NOT my favorite strategy.

For example, let's say that we were going to sell to the tenant buyer at $300,000, and they didn't purchase the property. We hired a Realtor, and we ended up only getting $290,000 from the sale, after paying all the commissions. That's $10,000 less than we were going to get from the tenant buyer. And if I were initially going to make $20,000 profit on this joint venture, I would lose $10,000 of profits because the agreement I have with my Joint Venture Investors is that any loss from the sale would be deducted from *my* earnings first.

Selling the property is an exit strategy that you should only look at in a good market. If it's a slow or down market, I will look at finding another tenant buyer, assuming, of course, that the existing tenant buyer doesn't want to extend, and that the investor doesn't want to extend.

I would then find another tenant buyer, and I would make the option price higher, depending on what the expected appreciation is. If the expected appreciation is not that high, I may increase the monthly payment to include some extra profit to make it worth it for the investor.

Check out **WWW.JIMPELLERIN.COM** for more articles on Lease Options and Real Estate Investing.

Chapter 12. Conclusion

That concludes our look at how to make money using Lease Options. It's an effective way to get involved in Real Estate without using any of your money.

We showed you three different Lease Option strategies: the property-first Lease Option, the tenant-first Lease Option, and the sandwich Lease Option.

We showed two different ways to acquire a property: 1) from a motivated seller or 2) by using an investor.

We showed you how to set up a joint venture.

We described all the different contracts and when to use them. We introduced the *Lease Agreement*, the *Option Agreement*, and an *Agreement of Purchase and Sale* and when to use each of them. We also described the *Joint Venture Agreement* and the *Property Management Agreement* and when to use each of those.

We showed you the four ways in which you can make your money in Lease Options: through the down payment, through the monthly payment, through the sale price, and through the mortgage principal paydown.

We talked about the different exit strategies: the tenant buys, extending the contract, finding another tenant buyer, or just selling.

A Lease Option is probably the easiest and best way to make money when working with single-family homes, or at least it's the easiest and best way that I've found to make money with single-family homes. Lease Options are perfect for the person who wants to get into Real Estate and doesn't want to invest any of their own money. Based on this, I wouldn't recommend putting any of your money down to purchase a property.

Instead, why wouldn't you go out and find a motivated seller or find an investor to joint venture with? You can do a lot more transactions when you are leveraging other people's money. And you don't personally have to qualify for any of these properties. You never have to get approved for a mortgage from the bank.

You can do 2 or 3 Lease Options a year if you want. Or you can do 10 or 20 Lease Options a year if you so choose. It depends on what your long-term goals are. Are you going to use Lease Option investing to supplement your income, or do you want to replace your income?

There's lots of money to be made doing Lease Options. Some people are even doing Lease

Options with high-end properties. Don't just think a Lease Option is for moderate to low-income people. Some people can't qualify for mortgages that have very high incomes.

For example, new immigrants to the country may want to buy a higher-priced home. I've seen people do a Lease Option with a $2M home. The reason is still the same.

The Tenant Buyer doesn't have credit, but they have high incomes. Maybe they make $1M a year, but their credit score is poor. The process is the same. You find a motivated seller who is trying to sell their expensive home, and you find the right tenant buyer.

There are not as many of these higher-priced transactions. And the way you would market more expensive homes is much different. Different channels would have to be used to find these high-income tenant buyers and motivated sellers with higher-priced homes.

It will take a lot longer to close a higher-priced transaction than it would for a lower-priced Lease Option deal. I can usually find tenant buyers in 30, 60, or 90 days at the most for the low-end deals. If you are trying to find a tenant buyer for a $1M home, it's probably going to take you closer to 6 months.

Hopefully, I have provided you with a lot of useful information for you to get started with Lease Options.

Go to my website WWW.JIMPELLERIN.COM and subscribe to my list. There's lots more information there and some free resources for you to use.

Good luck.

Check out **WWW.JIMPELLERIN.COM** for more articles on Lease Options and Real Estate Investing.

About The Author

JIM PELLERIN started real estate investing over twenty years ago. Since then, he has bought and sold millions of dollars of real estate. He began by purchasing and renting out duplexes. Recently he has added Lease Options to his strategy. He is currently acquiring two to four Lease Option properties a month. He has implemented many unique funding strategies that have allowed him to continue implementing his strategy and continue building his sizable portfolio.

As part of his education, he has attended numerous seminars on real estate investing, project management, property management, financing, renovations, motivation, time management, and many more. He has also read over 500 books on similar topics.

This book blends his experience and the knowledge he has gained through his investments and studies.

Check out **WWW.JIMPELLERIN.COM** for more articles on Lease Options and Real Estate Investing.

Other Books By Jim Pellerin

Real Estate Investing: Strategies – The Secret to Financial Independence with Real Estate

https://books2read.com/JimPellerin

Invest NOW – The Passive Approach to Winning with Real Estate

https://books2read.com/JimPellerin

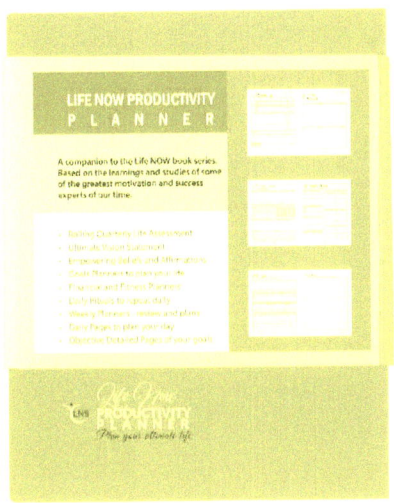

Life Now Productivity Planner

https://books2read.com/JimPellerin